Latitude Adjustments

Latitude Adjustments

Jimmy Buffett Quotes

for your daily dose of tropical wisdom

BEACH BUM BOOKS

Published by Beach Bum Books. First editition, 2024.

Beach Bum Books is a proud supporter of Save the Manatee Club, an award-winning national nonprofit and membership-based organization established in 1981 by the late renowned singer-songwriter, author, and entrepreneur Jimmy Buffett and former U.S. Senator Bob Graham when we was governor of Florida. Save the Manatee Club's mission is to protect manatees and their aquatic habitat. A portion of proceeds from all Beach Bum Books sales are donated to the organization.

www.BeachBumBooks.com

ISBN (paperback): 979-8-9913656-0-4
ISBN (hardcover): 979-8-9913656-1-1

For my mom, Doreen,
who raised me from a Parakeet to the Parrothead I am today.

Bubbles up!

Table of Contents

Introduction

Welcome, fellow Parrotheads, to *Latitude Adjustments: Jimmy Buffett Quotes for Your Daily Dose of Tropical Wisdom.* This collection is a heartfelt tribute to the man who has inspired countless sun-soaked days and breezy nights with his music, lyrics, and philosophy. Jimmy Buffett's songs have a way of transporting us to a world where the sun is always shining, the drinks are always cold, and worries are as fleeting as a summer breeze.

As a lifelong Parrothead, I've found immense joy and solace in Buffett's words. (And, I suppose if we're being particular, I started as a Parakeet.) His music has been a constant companion through life's ups and downs, reminding me to laugh, love, and embrace the moment. This book is a celebration of that spirit—a curated collection of quotes that capture the essence of Jimmy's wisdom and whimsy.

In *Latitude Adjustments*, you'll find quotes that touch on everything from the simple pleasures of a cheeseburger in paradise to the deeper reflections of life's changes and transitions. Each quote is accompanied by a blurb, offering a bit of inspiration, introspection, or just a good laugh.

Whether you're looking for a moment of escape, a nugget of wisdom, or a reason to smile, you'll find it here. Welcome to the world of Beach Bum Books—where every page is a step closer to paradise. Here's to living life with a little more sun, sea, and stories.

Bubbles up!

H.R. Gordon, Executive Beach Bum

Changes in Latitudes, Changes in Attitudes

Life is a continuous journey of changes and transitions, much like navigating through shifting latitudes. As we move through different phases, maintaining a sense of humor and a positive perspective can be our greatest allies.

This section explores the beauty and inevitability of change. Through reflections on life's whirlwinds, the importance of letting go, and the power of living authentically, these quotes remind us to embrace every twist and turn with grace and laughter. Whether it's adapting to new circumstances or finding peace in the chaos, the insights in this chapter encourage us to stay resilient and find joy in the ever-evolving adventure of life.

"It's those changes in latitudes, changes in attitudes; nothing remains quite the same. With all of our running and all of our cunning, if we couldn't laugh we would all go insane."

Changes in Latitudes, Changes in Attitudes (1977)

Life is a series of changes and adaptations, much like the shifting latitudes and attitudes Jimmy Buffett sings about. This quote reminds us that while everything around us may change, maintaining a sense of humor is crucial for navigating life's ups and downs.

Laughter can be a powerful coping mechanism, helping us stay sane amid the chaos of our busy lives. Reflect on a recent moment where laughter helped you overcome a difficult situation.

How can you bring more humor and lightness into your daily routine?

"I'm just hangin' on while this old world keeps spinning, and it's good to know it's out of my control. If there's one thing that I've learned from all this livin', is that it wouldn't change a thing if I let go."

Trip Around the Sun (2004)

Life often feels like a whirlwind, with many things spinning out of our control. This quote emphasizes the importance of acceptance and letting go of the need to control everything. By recognizing that we can't manage every aspect of our lives, we find peace and freedom.

Reflect on an area in your life where you've been trying to maintain control. Consider how letting go could bring relief and possibly open new doors. Trust in the flow of life and focus on what you can influence, allowing the rest to unfold naturally.

"Let those winds of time blow over my head.
I'd rather die while I'm living than live while I'm dead."

Growing Older But Not Up (1981)

Embrace the present and live life to the fullest. This lyric encourages us to prioritize truly living over merely existing. It's a call to seize the moment, take risks, and embrace experiences that make us feel alive.

Reflect on areas of your life where you might be playing it safe or holding back. How can you infuse more passion and adventure into your daily routine? Remember, life is meant to be lived with zest and enthusiasm. Don't let the fear of time passing hold you back. Instead, let it motivate you to make the most of every moment.

"Days precious days roll in and out like waves.
I got boards to bend I got planks to nail.
I got charts to make; I got seas to sail."

Boats to Build (2004)

The lyric captures the essence of time slipping by like waves, emphasizing the urgency of seizing each moment. It speaks to the endless tasks and dreams we all have—boards to bend, planks to nail, charts to make, and seas to sail. Life is filled with responsibilities and aspirations, reminding us to make the most of our precious days.

Reflect on how you spend your time. Are you balancing your daily tasks with your dreams and aspirations? Today, take a moment to focus on your own "boards to bend" and "seas to sail." Embrace the idea that every day is an opportunity to move closer to your goals while appreciating the journey. Use this reminder to stay motivated and ensure you're dedicating time to both your responsibilities and the things that truly matter to you.

"Nothing can tear you apart if you keep living straight from the heart. Though you know that you're gonna hurt some, the magic will come."

Bring Back the Magic (1988)

Living authentically and from the heart means embracing vulnerability and being true to yourself, even when it leads to moments of pain. This quote highlights that while staying true to your heart can expose you to hurt, it also opens the door to magical, transformative experiences.

Reflect on a time when being genuine brought you both challenges and joy. How can you continue to live authentically, trusting that the magic will come despite the occasional hurt?

"It's the prophecy of the unattainable dream.
If you take one look behind the shine,
it doesn't always gleam."

Diamond as Big as the Ritz (1995)

Chasing dreams often reveals that not everything is as perfect as it seems. Reflect on the dreams and goals you've pursued. How often have you found that reality didn't match your expectations? Today, embrace the journey itself, with all its flaws and surprises. Recognize that true fulfillment comes from the experiences and growth gained along the way, not from achieving an idealized perfection.

Appreciate the small victories and lessons learned, even when things don't gleam as brightly as you hoped. Embrace the imperfections and find joy in the present moment, knowing that the value lies in the journey, not just the destination.

"But now I'm incommunicado, drivin' by myself down the road with a hole in it. Songs with no vibrato, takin' the long way home."

Incommunicado (1981)

Reflect on the moments when you felt disconnected or needed time alone to think. How did those journeys shape your understanding of yourself and your path in life?

Embrace the idea of taking the long way home—allow yourself the time and space to reflect and find clarity. Whether it's a quiet drive, a walk, or simply sitting in a peaceful spot, use this time to reconnect with your thoughts and feelings.

Remember that these moments of solitude are valuable for personal growth and understanding, helping you navigate your way with renewed perspective and purpose.

"You and I, we can't change the weather, and we're all in this together, so let the strong wind blow. Oh now, things will be much better if you don't become a prisoner to the reason you should know."

Blue Guitar (2002)

Life's challenges are inevitable, and while we can't control everything, we can choose how we respond. This lyric highlights the importance of unity and resilience, reminding us that we're all in this together. It encourages us not to be confined by rigid thinking or overanalyzing but to embrace the winds of change with an open heart.

Reflect on how you handle situations beyond your control. Are there ways you can release the need to have all the answers? Focus on staying flexible and united with others as you navigate life's unpredictable moments. Embrace the strength that comes from community and let go of the need to control every outcome. Things will improve when you allow yourself to flow with the changes.

"A cup of coffee and a shaky hand. Waking up in a foreign land. Trying to act like I got something planned—that's my window on the world."

Window on the World (2004)

Navigating the unknown with a mix of curiosity and uncertainty is a familiar feeling. This lyric captures the essence of stepping into new experiences without a clear plan, relying on a cup of coffee and the thrill of discovery. It's about embracing the adventure of the unfamiliar.

Reflect on a time when you found yourself in a new situation, feeling unprepared yet excited. How did you adapt and find your way? Today, embrace the unpredictability of life. Allow yourself to wake up to new possibilities, even if you don't have everything figured out. Sometimes, the best views come from looking through an uncertain window on the world.

"Don't have to work it all out; don't have to tear it all apart.
All you need's a place to start. And if it never worked before,
try it just once more. That's what your heart is for."

Someday I Will (2002)

Starting something new can feel overwhelming, but you don't need to have it all figured out from the beginning. This lyric encourages us to take that first step, trusting that persistence and heart will guide us. It's about giving things another try, even if they didn't work out before.

Reflect on an area in your life where you've felt hesitant to begin or try again. How can you take that first step today?

Remember, your heart is there to support and guide you through uncertainty. Embrace the journey, knowing that every attempt is a valuable part of the process.

"Order to disorder, it's the way we all fly.
Light speed is all you need to pass the future by."

Einstein Was a Surfer (2013)

Life's journey often moves from order to disorder and back again, reflecting the natural ebb and flow of experiences. This lyric highlights the rapid pace of life and how quickly the future becomes the present. It's a reminder to embrace the chaos and speed of our journey.

Reflect on how you've navigated the swift changes in your life. Have you learned to adapt to the disorder? Today, embrace the fast pace and unpredictability of your journey. Understand that moving at light speed can bring you quickly into new experiences and opportunities. Trust the process and find balance in the constant flux, knowing that each moment propels you forward.

"But every now and then, the dragons come to call. Just when you least expect it, you'll be dodgin' cannonballs."

Jamaica Mistaica (1996)

Sometimes things don't work out the way you planned. Take Jimmy's trip to Jamaica for some chicken for example. Lunch doesn't usually end up in gunfire, but he turned "another shitty day in paradise" into yet another hit song.

Remember to take things in stride. Look for the simplest explanation in things. And turn your shitty days into something positive or productive.

Think about something that recently really annoyed or upset you. How can you turn that into something creative?

"Better days are in the cards, I feel.
I feel it in the changing winds."

Love and Luck (1992)

Optimism can be a powerful force, especially when you sense change in the air. This lyric speaks to the hope and anticipation that better days are ahead. It's a reminder to stay positive and trust that challenges will give way to brighter times.

Reflect on the moments when you've felt the winds of change in your life. How did you embrace the positivity and move forward?

Today, focus on the potential for good things to come. Trust in your intuition and the natural ebb and flow of life. Better days are indeed in the cards, waiting just around the corner.

"Why don't you wander and follow 'la vie dansante' on the night wind that takes you just where you want?"

La Vie Dansante (1979)

There's magic in letting go and allowing life to guide you. This lyric invites us to embrace spontaneity and the dance of life, trusting the journey to take us where we need to be. It's about the joy of exploration and the freedom of wandering with an open heart.

Reflect on moments when you've let go of control and allowed life to lead you. How did it feel to embrace the unknown?

Today, consider how you can incorporate more spontaneity and trust into your life. Follow the night wind, wander freely, and let La Vie Dansante—the dancing life—carry you to new and wonderful places.

"When you stop and think about it, life is still just high school. You make the same mistakes you did when you were young: contending for the ladies' favors, tasting every single flavor, while hopelessly trying not to scald your tongue."

Last Man Standing (2002)

Life has a funny way of circling back to familiar patterns. Despite the passage of time and the wisdom we gain, we continue to make similar mistakes, driven by the same desires and faced with recurring challenges.

Buffett's reflection is a gentle reminder of the timelessness of human experience. We vie for affection, explore new opportunities, and learn through inevitable missteps. His words invite us to view these patterns with humor and acceptance. Instead of seeing repeated mistakes as failures, we can recognize them as part of life's ongoing adventure.

Savor each moment, learn from our experiences, and appreciate the enduring nature of life's lessons.

"Life can be a pickle or a stalk of sugar cane."

Close Calls (2023)

This line reminds us that life is a blend of the sour and the sweet, with moments that challenge us and those that bring us joy. Just as a pickle's tartness can be surprising and sharp, some experiences can be difficult and demanding. On the other hand, like the sweetness of sugar cane, life also offers times of pleasure and delight.

The challenges we face can make the sweet moments even more meaningful, and the joys we encounter can give us strength to endure the tough times. By recognizing and accepting this balance, we can navigate life with greater resilience and appreciation.

Savor every part of your journey. Whether dealing with the sour or the sweet, each close call contributes to the richness of our lives, helping us grow and find deeper satisfaction in the everyday.

"Now great whales travel the rhumb lines, dodging those deadly harpoons. Spawning their young, as their ancestors done in the depths of her hidden lagoons. There're times I find myself with them, and times I feel as they do. We're on a similar course; it's just a different source, but I'm in danger of extinction too."

Treat Her Like A Lady (1979)

This imagery evokes a profound connection to nature and a sense of shared struggle for survival. Reflect on the parallels between the whales' journey and your own life. How do you navigate the dangers and challenges you face?

Today, take a moment to consider the paths you travel and the legacy you are creating. Embrace the idea that, like the whales, we are all on a journey that connects us to something greater. Recognize the importance of preserving and protecting not only our own well-being but also the natural world around us. By understanding our place in the larger ecosystem, we can find strength and purpose in our actions, ensuring that we and the world we cherish endure for generations to come.

"His world had gone from sailin' ships to rakin' mom's backyard. He never could adjust to land, although he tried so hard."

The Captain And The Kid (1976)

Written about his grandfather, this reflection reminds us of the challenges faced when moving away from a beloved way of life. The sea was more than just a job for the captain; it was his passion and identity. Trying to adapt to a landlocked life was difficult, if not impossible. Through the eyes of a grandchild, there's a deep appreciation for the captain's enduring spirit and the adventures that shaped him.

Consider the transitions in your own life and the challenges they bring. Reflect on how shifting from a beloved routine or passion can be both difficult and transformative. Embrace the idea that our passions continue to guide us, even when circumstances change dramatically.

"It's something more than DNA that tells us who we are
It's method and it's magic, we are of the stars."

Oysters and Peals (1999)

This sentiment explores the profound truth that our identity is shaped by more than just our genetic makeup. It's a blend of method and magic, a reminder that we are connected to something greater—the stars. This perspective encourages us to embrace the wonder and complexity of our existence, recognizing the beautiful interplay between science and mystery that defines who we are.

How can you appreciate the unique blend of factors that contribute to your identity, celebrating both the tangible and the magical aspects of your being?

"They were changin' channels, waitin' for their sails to fill.
They were changin' channels, always will."

Changing Channels (1989)

Embracing the ebb and flow of life, this sentiment highlights the
constant search for new directions and opportunities. Changing
channels while waiting for sails to fill signifies the ongoing jour-
ney of adaptation and exploration. It's a reminder that life is
full of transitions, and the ability to remain flexible and open to
new possibilities is essential. Maintaining a sense of humor and
perspective helps us navigate these changes with grace.

How can you stay adaptable and optimistic as you navigate
the ever-changing channels of your own life?

"So fellas, listen to my story now, though you have heard this tale before. Take care of your needs and watch out for your greeds, or that wolf will be at your door."

I Used To Have Money One Time (1983)

This cautionary tale emphasizes the importance of balance in life. Failing to do so can invite trouble. This sentiment encourages us to reflect on our priorities and ensure that we maintain a healthy balance between fulfilling our essential needs and avoiding excessive desires.

It's a timeless lesson that underscores the value of moderation and wisdom in navigating life's changes and challenges. How can you strike a balance in your own life to keep the wolf from your door?

"To my friends who are jolly—when melancholy knocks, sometimes they let her in to sit and share stories of flops and of glories—it ain't half as bad as the bends. Sometimes living's a struggle, multiplied double, but they love it too much for the party to end."

Bubbles Up (2023)

Embracing life's ups and downs with resilience, this sentiment captures the spirit of welcoming even the tough times with grace. When melancholy knocks, it's met with stories of both failures and triumphs, highlighting the full spectrum of human experience. Life's struggles may be challenging, but the love for living and the joy found in every moment keeps the party going.

This quote reminds us to appreciate the highs and endure the lows, finding strength and joy in the journey. How can you cultivate resilience and embrace the joy of life, no matter what challenges come your way?

"Sometimes I may get a little drastic. Sometimes I just let my
feelin's show. Sometimes I may be a bit sarcastic.
But most times that's the way the story goes."

Twelve Volt Man (1983)

Embracing the full range of emotions and expressions, this
sentiment highlights the importance of authenticity. Some-
times we may act drastically, let our feelings show, or be a bit
sarcastic, but that's just part of the human experience. Life's
story is often a mix of raw emotions and honest reactions.

This quote encourages us to accept our genuine selves, with
all our quirks and imperfections. How can you embrace your
true feelings and expressions, accepting them as a natural
part of your personal journey?

"All your life you have to deal with ups and downs, so listen to your heartstrings as they make the sounds. Don't forget to listen to that steady beat. Don't forget to balance on your ready feet."

Gravity Storm (1989)

Life is a continuous journey of ups and downs, and navigating it requires listening to your inner rhythm. Your heartstrings provide the sounds and guidance needed to maintain balance amidst the chaos. This sentiment emphasizes the importance of staying grounded and steady on your feet, finding harmony between your emotions and actions. It's a reminder to trust your heart and maintain balance, no matter the challenges you face.

How can you stay attuned to your inner voice and maintain equilibrium in the ever-changing landscape of life?

"You got to bend a little one way or the other. You got to leave
your mind open to discover. Seems I've been fightin' it all along.
You got to bend a little no matter which side you're on,
or soon you'll be gone."

Bend a Little (1975)

Flexibility and openness are key to navigating life's challenges.
This sentiment emphasizes the importance of bending a little,
keeping your mind open to new discoveries and perspectives.
The struggle to stay rigid can be exhausting, and adapting is
crucial, no matter your stance. Embracing this flexibility en-
sures resilience and longevity.

How can you incorporate openness and adaptability into your life,
allowing you to grow and thrive amidst changing circumstances?

"She has worn a wealth of costumes—hula skirts to wedding gowns. Lived in cities walked through jungles—always sees the sun go down."

Hula Girl at Heart (2006)

The value of adapting to life's changes and appreciating varied experiences shines through her journey. By welcoming new adventures and cherishing different chapters, one can gain a deeper understanding and joy. Each role and place our Hula Girl encounters adds to her life's richness, creating a beautiful mosaic of experiences. The peace found in watching the sun set each day serves as a reminder of the beauty in transition and the constancy of nature's rhythms.

How can you open yourself to new experiences and find beauty in the ever-changing moments of life, creating your own tapestry of memories and understanding?

"And one way or the other we're all refugees livin' out this easy life below the banyan trees, smoothing off the rougher edges of the culture clash. We've got a style. We've got a look. We've got that old panache."

Everybody's Got a Cousin in Miami (1994)

In many ways, we're all refugees, seeking solace and simplicity under the shade of banyan trees. Embracing this existence fosters a sense of unity and individuality, blending diverse influences into a harmonious way of life.

How can you adapt to the changing landscapes around you, finding peace and expressing your unique style amidst life's complexities?

"I'm the type of guy who likes it right down the middle; I don't like all this bouncing back and forth. Me, I want to live with my feet in Dixie and my head in the cool blue north."

Nothin' But a Breeze (2006)

Some prefer balance over constant change, seeking a life that combines the best of both worlds. This creates harmony and reflects a longing for stability with a perfect blend of contrasting experiences.

How can you create a life that balances different elements, providing both comfort and adventure, warmth and tranquility? Finding your unique equilibrium can lead to a fulfilling and enriched life.

Cheeseburger in Paradise

Life's simplest pleasures often bring the greatest joy. In this section, we celebrate those indulgent moments that make life deliciously worthwhile.

Inspired by Jimmy Buffett's whimsical approach to enjoying every bite and every moment, these quotes remind us to savor the small things that bring happiness. Whether it's the taste of a favorite food or the joy of a little rebellion, these reflections encourage us to find delight in the everyday. Embrace the tart and the sweet, the indulgent and the simple, as we explore the joys of living a life full of flavor.

"Making the best of every virtue and vice. Worth every damn bit of sacrifice to get a cheeseburger in paradise."

Cheeseburger in Paradise (1978)

This whimsical ode to the simple pleasures in life reminds us that sometimes, joy comes in the form of small, everyday indulgences. Jimmy always asserted that this song had no ulterior motives, so let's not think to deep about the philosophy here. Just enjoy the simple things.

Life is a series of choices and sacrifices, and sometimes, a bit of indulgence is worth it. So, savor those moments that bring you pure, uncomplicated joy—like biting into a perfect cheeseburger in your own paradise.

"If you're gonna fly high without fear you're gonna have to learn to love the atmosphere, and you gotta learn to use those wings that you can't see."

Wings (2009)

Embracing life's adventures often means stepping into the unknown, a leap that requires courage and trust. Buffett's words encourage us to soar high and embrace the journey, even when the path isn't visible.

Learning to love the atmosphere—the challenges and uncertainties—becomes essential. It's about trusting in our invisible wings, our innate strengths and resilience, to guide us. So, let's embrace our fears, spread our wings, and take flight, knowing that the invisible forces within us will help us navigate the skies of life.

"It's crazy and it's different, but it's really being free.
And reasons the world would want to question,
makes sense to you and me."

Livingston's Gone to Texas (1975)

This lyric captures the essence of embracing a lifestyle that is unconventional yet liberating. It's about finding freedom in the craziness and different paths we choose, even when the world questions our choices.

This reflection reminds us that true freedom often lies in stepping away from societal norms and embracing what makes us truly happy. The reasons behind our choices may not always make sense to others, but they resonate deeply with us.

Consider what unconventional choices have brought you joy and freedom. How can you continue to embrace the "crazy and different" in your life?

"Mademoiselle, voulez-vous danser? A new moon has come
out to play. Take my hand, step outside.
These doors and windows open wide."

Mademoiselle (2002)

Embracing the spontaneity and magic of life is about taking chances and stepping outside your comfort zone. Reflect on the last time you allowed yourself to be swept away by the moment. When did you last take a chance and step outside your comfort zone?

Today, invite a bit of spontaneity into your life. Whether it's a dance under the stars, a walk in the moonlight, or simply opening your heart to new experiences, let yourself be guided by the magic of the moment. Embrace the idea that life's most beautiful moments often come when we least expect them, and allow yourself to be open to the possibilities that await.

"Commit a little mortal sin.
It's good for the soul."

Graefruit - Juicy Fruit (1973)

This lighthearted take on indulging in small transgressions speaks to the idea that a little rebellion can be revitalizing. In a world often governed by rigid rules and expectations, allowing ourselves the freedom to step outside the lines can bring a refreshing sense of liberation and joy.

Buffett's words suggest that these minor acts of defiance are not just harmless fun but are beneficial for our well-being. They remind us to embrace our human imperfections and to occasionally break away from the constraints of routine and conformity. By doing so, we reconnect with our true selves and find balance in our lives.

"'Cause I'm livin' on things that excite me—be they pastry or lobster or love. I'm just tryin' to get by bein' quiet and shy in a world full of pushin' and shove."

The Wino and I Know (1974)

Living in a world that often feels like it's rushing by at breakneck speed, it's easy to get caught up in the hustle. But Buffett reminds us to savor the simple pleasures, whether it's the delight of a pastry, the luxury of lobster, or the warmth of love.

Embracing the things that excite us can bring joy and meaning to our lives, even if we're naturally quiet and shy. In a society that values noise and aggression, finding contentment in the little things can be a quiet rebellion against the chaos. So, let's cherish those moments of joy and let them carry us through the push and shove of the world.

"Spend it while you can, money's contraband.
You can't take it with you when you go."

Carnival World (1989)

Life is fleeting, and money is just a tool. This lyric reminds us that we can't take wealth with us when we go, so it's best to spend it while we can.

Reflect on how you use your resources. Are you saving for a distant future or enjoying the present? Today, consider treating yourself or others to something special. Embrace the idea that money is meant to enhance our lives, not just accumulate.

Find a balance between saving responsibly and spending joyfully. By doing so, you can create memorable experiences and enrich your life and the lives of those around you, making the most of the time and resources you have.

"I never thought of life as being breezy. I never thought of time as time to play. I never thought that I could take it easy, but all those feelings changed for me today."

Island Fever (1998)

Sometimes, a shift in perspective can transform how we view life. This lyric speaks to the realization that life can be enjoyed with ease and playfulness. It's about breaking free from old habits of stress and seriousness to embrace a more relaxed and joyful approach to living.

Reflect on the moments that have shifted your perspective on life. What experiences have helped you see the value in taking it easy and enjoying the present? Today, allow yourself to embrace a breezier, more playful attitude. Let go of unnecessary stress and find joy in the simplicity of the moment. Remember, it's never too late to change how you experience life.

"Ain't it crazy how something seems like nothing at all. Take a big old room make it seem so small. Seeing windows where there are walls makes a whole lot of something out of nothing at all."

Somethin' Bout a Boat (2013)

Perspective can transform our reality. What seems insignificant can become meaningful when viewed through a different lens. This lyric reminds us that our outlook can turn empty spaces into cozy nooks and barriers into opportunities.

Reflect on a time when a change in perspective shifted your view of a situation. How can you apply this mindset to your current challenges? Today, try to see windows where there are walls and find the hidden potential in everyday moments. Embrace the power of perspective to make a whole lot of something out of nothing at all.

"The jungle drums are beating with the tales from late last night.
'Cause stories bear repeating for everyone's delight."

Coconut Telegraph (1981)

There's a unique joy in sharing stories, especially the ones filled with a little gossip. The jungle drums beating with tales from the previous night remind us how stories bring people together, sparking laughter and delight.

Gossip, when lighthearted, can be a source of camaraderie and entertainment. It's about connecting over shared moments and reliving the humor and excitement of events.

These stories, retold with enthusiasm, weave a sense of community and shared joy. How can you find delight in the playful retelling of last night's adventures?

"We ain't got no money, we ain't got no right,
but we're gypsies in the palace, we got it all tonight."

Gypsies in the Palace (1985)

This lyric speaks to the spirit of living in the moment and finding joy in what we have, no matter how little. It's about embracing spontaneity and the thrill of freedom, making the best of our circumstances. Sometimes, the most unforgettable nights come from the simplest pleasures and the wild, carefree adventures we share with friends.

Reflect on a time when you felt truly free and alive, regardless of your circumstances. How can you capture that gypsy spirit in your everyday life? Remember, it's the experiences and connections that make us feel rich, not material possessions.

"Oh I am still a child when it comes to something wild."

The Night I Painted the Sky (1995)

There's a part of us that remains untouched by time—the inner child that revels in spontaneity and adventure. This quote reminds us to embrace that youthful spirit and remain open to wild, untamed experiences.

Reflect on what makes you feel alive and free, like a child discovering the world for the first time. How can you incorporate more of that wild, joyful energy into your daily life?

Let your inner child guide you toward moments of uninhibited joy and wonder.

"When you're back at work at your 9 to 5, and it's pourin' rain on your mornin' drive, you'll remember when you were last alive down at the lah de dah."

Down at the Lah De Dah (2020)

Think back to those moments when you felt most alive. What were you doing? Where were you? Use these memories as a source of inspiration during mundane days. They remind us to seek balance, to infuse our daily lives with joy and adventure.

Today, take a moment to reconnect with those feelings of freedom and happiness. Whether it's through a small adventure, a new experience, or simply reminiscing about past joys, let these memories brighten your routine. Embrace the idea that while responsibilities are a part of life, making space for moments that make us feel alive is essential for a fulfilling life.

"Beneath the moonlit sky, shadows walk beside the water. Sad good-bye whispered on the shore; hear those wind chimes play, they serenade the shadow lovers. Ring and fade away like California promises."

California Promises (1983)

Take time to savor the small, ephemeral joys that come your way. By acknowledging the impermanence of these moments, you can find deeper meaning and connection in the here and now, allowing yourself to fully experience the serenade of life's fleeting beauty.

Reflect on the transient moments in your life that, like shadows and wind chimes, appear briefly and then disappear. How have these fleeting experiences shaped your understanding of love and loss? Today, embrace the beauty of the present, even knowing it may be temporary. Cherish the moments that feel like promises, and let their memory enrich your life.

"The place down the block—the one with no clock. Covert rendezvous with you at the usual time. I savor the scent of the fish on the grill. Life's so spicy up on Barbecue Hill. Looking good, you look so fine. Waiter, bring us one more bottle of wine."

I Wish Lunch Could Last Forever (1989)

There's a special charm in the familiar rituals of life, like meeting at a favorite spot with no clock to worry about. The joy of covert rendezvous and the savory scents capture the essence of life's simple pleasures.

A great atmosphere, combined with good company and a fine bottle of wine, celebrates the richness of these moments. It's a reminder to indulge in the flavors and experiences that make life delightful. How can you embrace and savor the simple joys and rituals that bring spice to your life?

"Cookin' is a pleasure; singin' is a treasure that most don't find. There ain't no harm in tellin' I likes to eat my melon right on down to the rind."

Homemade Music (1988)

Celebrating the simple joys of life, this sentiment highlights the pleasures of cooking and singing—treasures that bring immense satisfaction. Savoring every bit of a melon, right down to the rind, reflects a zest for life's simple pleasures. It's a reminder that happiness can be found in everyday activities and that there's no harm in enjoying them to the fullest.

How can you embrace and find joy in the simple, everyday pleasures that make life rich and fulfilling?

"In the mornin' when you rise, aren't you glad to be alive?
Oh oh put on your barefoot shoes when you dance
beneath the moon rainbow."

Why the Things We Do (1989)

Celebrating the simple pleasures of life, this sentiment captures the joy of waking up each morning and feeling grateful to be alive. Putting on your barefoot shoes and dancing beneath the moon rainbow evokes a sense of carefree happiness and connection with nature.

It's a reminder to embrace the small, delightful moments that bring joy and wonder to our everyday lives. How can you find and celebrate these simple pleasures, infusing your days with gratitude and light-heartedness?

"My garden is filled with papayas and mangos.
My life is a mixture of reggaes and tangos.
Taste for the good life—I can't live it no other way."

Lone Palm (1994)

Embracing the lushness of a life filled with tropical fruits and vibrant music, this sentiment captures the joy of living fully and savoring the good life. With a garden bursting with papayas and mangos and a soundtrack of reggaes and tangos, there's an undeniable zest for life's pleasures. It's a celebration of indulgence and the richness of diverse experiences, affirming that living well is the only way to live.

How can you cultivate a life filled with the flavors and rhythms that bring you the most joy?

"It could be it's that sausage or those pretty pink shrimp or that popcorn rice that makes me blow up like a blimp. Maybe it's that voodoo from Marie Laveau, but I will play for gumbo."

I Will Play for Gumbo (1999)

There's a playful willingness to do just about anything for the simple pleasure of a delicious bowl of gumbo. Whether it's the sausage, pink shrimp, or that mysterious voodoo from Marie Laveau, the joy of indulging in such a delightful dish is irresistible. It's a celebration of the lengths we'll go to for the things we love.

What's your gumbo? What are you willing to do to get it? Embrace the fun and determination in pursuing the simple pleasures that bring you happiness.

"Need is a relative thing these days; it borders on desire.
The high-tech world is full of bright, shiny things
we think that we really require."

Tonight I Just Need My Guitar (2002)

In a world filled with bright, shiny new tech, it's easy to blur the lines between need and desire. We often convince ourselves that we require more than we actually do. This sentiment calls us to embrace simplicity and question how much of the latest technology we really need. It's a reminder to focus on the simple pleasures that bring true joy and contentment.

How can you simplify your life, cutting through the noise of consumerism to find genuine happiness in the essentials?

One Particular Harbour

Finding a sanctuary, a place where you feel at peace and truly at home, is essential for the soul. This section draws inspiration from Jimmy Buffett's lyrical odes to such harbors of tranquility and belonging.

Through these quotes, we reflect on the beauty of nature, the rhythms of a simpler life, and the comfort of cherished identities. Whether it's a serene landscape or a moment of uninterrupted connection with loved ones, these reflections remind us to seek and create our own harbors of happiness. Embrace the sense of peace and community that comes from finding your particular harbor in the vast ocean of life.

"I used to rule my world from a pay phone, ships out on the sea,
but now times are rough, and I got too much stuff.
Can't explain likes of me."

One Particular Harbour (1983)

Embrace the present moment and reflect on the past. Once, simplicity reigned—a pay phone and the open sea were all that was needed to feel in control. Now, the world has become more complex, and possessions can feel overwhelming. This sentiment speaks to the universal challenge of adapting to change and finding balance amidst life's chaos.

Remember the importance of letting go of the unnecessary and focusing on what truly brings joy and meaning. How can you simplify your life and rediscover the freedom and contentment of earlier days?

"Staring at a starry night sky dreaming up some place to go. 'Til that day comes, I'll be there alone without a care."

Nobody From Nowhere (2009)

Dreaming of future adventures can be a comforting escape, but there's also beauty in enjoying the present moment. This lyric reminds us that while we wait for our dreams to unfold, we can find peace and contentment in simply being.

Reflect on your own dreams and the places you envision yourself going. How can you balance those aspirations with an appreciation for where you are now? Today, allow yourself to dream under the starry sky but also find joy in the present. Embrace the calm and carefreeness of the moment, knowing that your dreams are on the horizon.

"There's a highway of stars across the heavens. There's a whispering song of the wind in the grass. There's a rolling thunder across the savannah. A hope and a dream at the edge of the sky, and your life is the story of the wind."

Great Heart (1988)

The natural world's beauty and mystery remind us that our lives are intertwined with the wonders around us. The stars, the wind, the thunder—all are part of a greater story, just as our hopes and dreams are part of our personal journey. Embracing this connection can inspire us to live fully and fearlessly.

Reflect on how nature influences and parallels your own story. What dreams are you chasing at the edge of the sky? How can you listen to the 'whispering song' of your own aspirations and let them guide you? Remember, your life is as dynamic and powerful as the wind.

"My personal utopia—a place to run to, where I can hide away. Where I can truly reign supreme, somewhere fresh and clean, where a man can dream."

King of Somewhere Hot (1988)

Everyone needs a sanctuary, a personal utopia where they can escape and rejuvenate. This lyric speaks to the longing for a place that offers peace, clarity, and the freedom to dream without constraints. It's about finding that special spot where you feel truly in control and at ease.

Reflect on your personal utopia. Where do you go to find peace and inspiration? How can you create more moments of sanctuary in your daily life? Today, take time to nurture your dreams and find spaces that allow you to feel fresh, clean, and supreme. Everyone deserves a place where they can truly reign and dream.

"Fun tickets in my pocket, visions in my brain.
Grandfather always told me if I went down, I might never come
back again. I studied the language tapes and I read all the books.
Still nothing prepared me for my very first look."

First Look (1986)

This song tells the story of Buffett's first visit to Rio de Janeiro
and how he fell in love with the city, well, at first look. This senti-
ment captures the essence of stepping into the unknown, where
preparation meets the reality of the moment. It reminds us that
true understanding comes from lived experiences and that even
the wisest advice can't fully prepare us for what lies ahead.

Embrace the excitement of new journeys and the lessons they
bring. How can you open yourself to the uncharted territories
in your life, ready to learn and grow from each new experience?

"The night was filled with magic, they bid the sea goodbye. They swam into the heavens; they stayed up in the sky. And all the island people when they wish upon a star see the dolphin and the Jolly Mon who tell 'em where they are."

Jolly Mon Sing (1985)

Enchanted nights carry a certain magic, like the tale of a dolphin and a Jolly Mon who swam into the heavens. Their story, filled with wonder, brings comfort and guidance to island people who look to the stars for direction.

This whimsical narrative reminds us of the power of dreams and the sense of connection to something greater than ourselves. It's a celebration of mystical journeys and the belief that the universe has a way of guiding us, if we just look up and believe. How can you tap into the magic of your own dreams and find direction in the stars above?

"My old red bike gets me around to the bars and the beaches of
my town, and there aren't many reasons I would leave.
Yes, I have found me some peace."

I Have Found Me a Home (1973)

Finding peace often lies in the simple pleasures of life, like
riding an old red bike around town. This sense of content-
ment comes from the freedom to explore familiar bars and
beaches, savoring the charm of your surroundings. It's about
embracing a slower pace and finding joy in everyday mo-
ments. When you discover such tranquility, there are few rea-
sons to seek it elsewhere.

This sentiment encourages us to appreciate the comfort and
peace found in our local haunts and routines. How can you
find and cherish the simple pleasures in your life, creating
your own sense of peace and contentment?

"Then they spied an island rise out of the sea. They fell back to Earth just as free as you please. The children all gathered, the church bells did ring. Suddenly, everyone started to sing"

Chanson Pour Les Petits Enfants (1979)

A song meant for the little children, as the title and chorus say, captures the whimsy and magic of childhood. As an island rises from the sea, a sense of wonder fills the air. The children gather, church bells ring, and everyone joins in joyful song, celebrating the adventure and freedom of returning home.

This enchanting moment reflects the simple joys and boundless imagination of youth. Embrace the playful spirit and the joy of shared experiences that make childhood so special. How can you keep the wonder and whimsy of childhood alive in your heart and in the lives of those around you?

"Feels nice to be home for awhile.
Let's sip champagne till we break into smiles."

Survive (1979)

There's a special kind of peace in coming home and find-ing sanctuary in familiar surroundings. Sipping champagne and sharing smiles captures the essence of this serene joy. It's about relishing the comfort and warmth of home, cel-ebrating the moments of togetherness that bring genuine happiness.

This sentiment reminds us to appreciate the simple pleasures and the sense of belonging that home provides. How can you create and savor these moments of peace and joy in your own life?

"Those crazy martian days when we went separate ways; through time and space we'd find a place to bring our lives in phase. We're lost amid the galaxies revolving, and we're all just a part of what's evolving."

Come to the Moon (1984)

Reflecting on the vastness of time and space, this sentiment captures the journey of finding a place where our lives align. Despite going separate ways, there's a sense of belonging and connection that transcends the cosmos. Amidst the galaxies and the ever-evolving universe, we seek out moments of harmony and sanctuary.

This quote reminds us that even in the vastness of existence, we are part of a larger whole, continually evolving and finding our place. How can you find peace and a sense of belonging in the midst of life's ever-changing journey?

"Blue light guitars and tropical breeze. Hummingbirds mime the words as they dance in the trees. It's a flashback kind of crowd; it's a cabaret sound. There's still some magic left in this tourist town."

Blue Heaven Rendezvous (1995)

Capturing the enchanting essence of Blue Heaven, a beloved restaurant in Key West, this imagery evokes a sense of timeless charm. The enduring magic of Blue Heaven is a reminder of the joy and tranquility found in special places that offer a sense of sanctuary.

This sentiment highlights the importance of finding places that offer a sense of peace and belonging. How can you discover and cherish those magical spots that bring tranquility and joy to your life?

"The sound of the low tide, the smell of the rain. Travelin' alone on my boat and my plane. Take it all in it's as big as it seems. Count all your blessings and remember your dreams."

Jimmy Dreams (1995)

Embracing the serene moments of life, this sentiment captures the essence of finding peace and wonder in the world around you. Whether traveling solo or exploring new horizons, there's a profound beauty in the quiet sounds and scents of nature. It's a reminder to appreciate the vastness of life, count your blessings, and keep your dreams alive.

How can you find tranquility and inspiration in the simple, yet profound moments of your journey, nurturing your dreams along the way?

"The ocean's always been my mother; salt water is the perfect cure.
But now my home break's on a website, that's got me thinkin' Ecuador."

Hey, That's My Wave (2020)

The ocean has always been a source of comfort and heal-
ing, like a nurturing mother, with salt water as the perfect
cure. But as familiar surf spots become increasingly pop-
ular online, the lure of uncharted waters grows stronger.
This sentiment captures the desire to find new, untouched
places and the eternal quest for serenity and solitude.

How can you embrace change and seek out new adventures
while holding onto the timeless comforts that have always
brought you peace?

"I want to dance with circus gypsies, talk with hippies, where the past and the future still walk down that same sandy street. The importance of elsewhere is still that important to me."

I Want to Go Back to Cartagena (2013)

Embracing the spirit of adventure and the allure of unique experiences, this sentiment captures the desire to dance with circus gypsies and converse with hippies on a timeless sandy street. It reflects the importance of finding special places where the past and future blend seamlessly, creating a sense of peace and belonging. The magic of "elsewhere" remains essential, reminding us that these journeys and discoveries enrich our lives and provide sanctuary for our souls.

How can you seek out your own "elsewhere," a place that offers both adventure and tranquility, where you feel truly at home?

"There are waves outside my window; there are airplanes in the sky; there are ships on the horizon, and a beach always nearby. Fish tacos on the table, no surfer can resist. How did I get this lucky?"

Who Gets to Live Like This (2020)

Life is full of beautiful moments and small blessings that we sometimes take for granted. Whether it's the view outside your window, the food on your table, or the simple pleasures of everyday life, there's so much to appreciate. This sentiment encourages us to reflect on our good fortune and cherish the unique experiences that make our lives special.

How can you cultivate a deeper sense of gratitude for the simple yet extraordinary aspects of your own life?

"Back when nature ruled the heavens, oh gypsies, fools, and loons
were dragged across the ocean by that everlasting moon"

Everlasting Moon (1992)

Reflecting on a time when nature held sway over the heav-
ens, this sentiment captures the adventurous spirit of those
who journeyed across the ocean, guided by the enduring
pull of the moon. It speaks to the timeless allure of explora-
tion and the natural forces that inspire human curiosity and
wanderlust. These adventurers, drawn by the everlasting
moon, found solace and inspiration in the journey itself.

Embrace this sense of adventure and connection to nature, al-
lowing it to guide you to your own peaceful harbor and enrich
your journey through life. How can you find your own mo-
ments of tranquility and adventure, letting nature's rhythms
lead you to new discoveries and a deeper sense of peace?

"I'm about a mile high in Denver, where the rock meets timberline.
Where God and trees create the breeze; tonight I'll call it mine."

A Mile High in Denver (1970)

High in Denver, where the rugged Rockies meet the tim-
berline, there's a special place where nature's beauty is
unparalleled. The blend of majestic trees and the divine
breeze creates a perfect sanctuary. As you breathe in the
crisp mountain air and take in the stunning scenery, this se-
rene moment becomes yours to cherish for the night. This
sentiment captures the essence of finding peace and a sense
of belonging in nature's embrace.

How can you seek out and cherish such tranquil moments,
letting them bring you a deep sense of peace and connec-
tion to the natural world, reminding you of the simple yet
profound joys that life offers?

"Island, I see you in the moonlight—silhouettes of ships in the night just make me want that much more."

Island (1981)

Under the moonlight, the island's silhouette and the passing ships evoke a longing for adventure and serenity. This enchanting vision fills your dreams, sparking a desire to one day explore its distant shores. The island represents hope, aspiration, and the promise of tranquility.

How can you keep your dreams alive and work towards reaching the places that call to your soul, finding peace and fulfillment along the way?

"I got a school boy heart, a novelist eye, stout sailor's legs, and a license to fly. I came with nomad feet and some wandering toes that glide up my longboard and hang off the nose."

School Boy Heart (1996)

With a school boy heart and a novelist's eye, there's an adventurous spirit that blends curiosity and creativity. Stout sailor's legs and a license to fly speak to the resilience and freedom found in exploration. Nomad feet and wandering toes glide up your longboard and hang off the nose, embodying the joy of surfing and the thrill of the unknown.

Embrace the essence of a life lived with a sense of adventure and a love for the sea. How can you tap into your own adventurous spirit, finding joy and fulfillment in exploration and new experiences?

"Well, I'm a tidal pool explorer from the days of my misspent youth. I believe that down on the beach, where the seagulls preach is where the Chinese buried the truth."

Coastal Confessions (2004)

From the adventurous days of youth, the beach has always been a place of exploration and discovery. Whether exploring tidal pools or listening to the calls of seagulls, there's a unique kind of wisdom found in these coastal moments. This connection to the shore and its mysteries embodies a lifelong pursuit of truth and adventure. The beach serves as a reminder that there are always new discoveries to be made and secrets to uncover.

How can you continue to embrace this spirit of exploration, seeking out hidden truths and finding wisdom in the world around you, wherever you may be?

"It's the small, small problems that keep me so upset and send me seeking shelter beneath my mosquito net. I stay there for hours, protected from the night, all those insects and vipers, and other things that bite."

Mental Floss (1996)

It's often the small, everyday problems that cause the most stress, driving us to seek a peaceful refuge. Beneath the safety of a mosquito net, you find a sanctuary from the night's nuisances—pesky insects, slithering vipers, and other things that bite. This haven becomes a personal harbor, shielding you from the chaos outside and offering a moment of tranquility.

How can you create your own serene retreat, a place where you can escape from life's minor troubles and find a sense of peace and protection? By carving out these sanctuaries, we allow ourselves the space to breathe and rejuvenate, ready to face the world again.

"Lying next to her by the ocean, reaching out and touching her hand. Whispering your secret emotion; magic in a magical land."

Mozambique (2023)

These moments by the sea encapsulate the serene and intimate connections that make life so special. These experiences remind us of the profound joy found in quiet, shared moments by the sea. The rhythmic sound of the waves, the feel of the sand, and the warmth of a shared touch all contribute to a timeless sense of tranquility and connection.

In these precious times, we find a deeper understanding of ourselves and our relationships, discovering the true essence of happiness and contentment. How can you cultivate more of these peaceful, magical experiences in your everyday life, creating lasting memories that enrich your journey?

Wastin' Away Again...

In the midst of life's hustle and bustle, there's an oasis of calm and joy where time seems to stand still. This section invites you to explore the essence of relaxation and escape.

Through these quotes, we delve into moments of serenity by the sea, the simple pleasure of unwinding, and the beauty of living in the present. Whether it's the allure of palm trees or the magic of a peaceful retreat, these reflections encourage us to take a step back and enjoy the bliss of doing nothing. Let go of your worries and immerse yourself in the laid-back spirit of Margaritaville.

"Don't know the reason I stayed here all season, nothin' to show but this brand new tattoo. But it's a real beauty, a Mexican cutie. How it got here I haven't a clue."

Margaritaville (1977)

Sometimes, the best stories come from the most unplanned moments, leaving us with memories and mementos that tell tales of laughter, mystery, and a touch of recklessness. That new tattoo, a symbol of a carefree season, might not have a clear origin, but it carries the spirit of the journey.

Embrace the unexpected twists and turns in your own life—they often lead to the most memorable and beautiful experiences. What unplanned adventures have brought you the greatest joy?

"I want to go back to the islands where the shrimp boats are tied up to the piling. Give me oysters and beer for dinner every day of the year, and I'll feel fine."

Tin Cup Chalice (1974)

Buffett's lyrics evoke a longing for a simpler, more relaxed way of life, where the sea provides both sustenance and serenity. It's a reminder of the healing power of nature and the joy found in life's simple pleasures. Sometimes, the hustle and bustle of daily life can make us yearn for a return to our roots, where the pace is slower and the days are savored.

Reflect on what 'island' represents for you—a place or state of mind where you find peace and happiness. How can you bring more of that simplicity and contentment into your daily routine?

"Sail away for a month at a time; sail away I've got to recharge
mind, then you'll find me back at it again."

Landfall (1977)

There's a rejuvenating power in taking a break and sailing
away, whether literally or metaphorically. A retreat to re-
charge the mind can work wonders, offering a fresh perspec-
tive and renewed energy. This idea underscores the impor-
tance of self-care and the necessity of stepping back to truly
come back stronger.

Embrace the opportunity to disconnect, find peace, and re-
turn with a refreshed spirit. How can you carve out time for
yourself to recharge and come back with renewed vigor?

"Everyone here is just more than contented to be
livin' and dyin' in three-quarter time."

Nautical Wheelers (1974)

Life has its own rhythm, and sometimes the sweetest moments are found in the slower, simpler beats. Buffett's lyric reminds us of the joy in taking things at a relaxed pace, finding contentment in the everyday flow. It's about appreciating where we are, rather than constantly chasing where we think we should be.

Reflect on a moment when you felt at peace, simply enjoying life as it came. How can you bring more of that three-quarter time rhythm into your daily routine? Embrace the ease and grace of living fully in the present.

"Life is always better when you add a little island,
a lot of oysters, love and wine."

Portugal Or PEI (2023)

Sometimes, the best things in life are the simplest pleasures. This lyric captures the essence of adding a touch of island spirit, good food, love, and wine to elevate our everyday experiences. It's a reminder that the little joys can make life infinitely richer and more enjoyable.

Reflect on the simple pleasures that bring you happiness. How can you incorporate more of these elements into your daily life? Today, add a little island spirit to your routine, whether it's through a favorite meal, spending time with loved ones, or enjoying a glass of wine. Embrace the idea that life is better with a touch of indulgence and a lot of love.

"Palm trees and views I can't believe. Why would I ever want to
leave? I think I'll take my shoes off and go walking
down beside the Caribbean Sea."

Island Fever (1998)

The allure of palm trees and breathtaking views makes it hard
to imagine leaving such a paradise. There's a sense of tranquil-
ity and wonder that comes with being in a place so beautiful.

Reflect on the last time you felt truly at peace in a special place.
What made it so memorable? Today, imagine yourself taking
off your shoes and walking beside the Caribbean Sea, feeling
the sand between your toes and the gentle waves lapping at your
feet. Embrace the idea of finding moments of serenity and joy,
whether in your surroundings or within yourself. These mo-
ments remind us of the beauty in the world and the importance
of taking time to appreciate it. Let yourself be present and en-
joy the simple pleasures that life has to offer.

"I'd like to go where the pace of life's slow, could you beam me somewhere, Mister Scotty? Any old place here on Earth or in space, you pick the century and I'll pick the spot."

Boat Drinks (1979)

There's a longing for simplicity and a slower pace in life, perfectly captured in this whimsical wish to be transported to a place where time moves gently. Whether it's a serene corner of Earth or a peaceful spot in the cosmos, the desire to escape the hustle and bustle is universal.

This playful appeal to be beamed away reflects a yearning for tranquility and the freedom to explore different times and places. It's a reminder to seek out moments of calm and find your personal paradise, wherever that may be. Where would you go to find your own slice of peace?

"Livin' for the weekend, jumpin' off the deep end with just enough money to buy a license to chill—and I believe I will."

License to Chill (2004)

This song celebrates the joy of living for the weekend and finding those precious moments to unwind and escape the daily grind. It's about making the most of your free time, prioritizing relaxation, and allowing yourself the luxury of a break.

Embrace the spirit of taking a step back, letting go of stress, and enjoying life's simple pleasures. Whether it's through a fun activity or just relaxing with friends, remember the importance of recharging your spirit. How can you create your own moments of relaxation and fun, ensuring you make the most of your time off?

"You're caught up in the internet, you think it's such a great asset, but you're wrong, wrong, wrong. All that fiberoptic gear still cannot take away the fear like an island song."

Holiday (1996)

The allure of the internet and its endless assets can be captivating, but it often falls short of addressing deeper emotional needs. Despite all the fiberoptic gear, it can't soothe fears or bring the same peace as a simple island song. This sentiment encourages us to unplug and find relaxation in timeless, uncomplicated pleasures.

How can you disconnect from the digital world and embrace the simple joys that offer true peace and relaxation?

"Don't know where I'm going, don't know where I've been. All I know for certain is my gummie just, my gummie just, my gummie just kicked in."

My Gummie Just Kicked In (2023)

Sometimes, life is about embracing the unknown and simply enjoying the ride. You might not know where you're going or where you've been, but moments of unexpected joy can make the journey delightful. When the effects of a gummie kick in, it's a reminder to relax and savor the present. This sentiment encourages letting go, unwinding, and finding happiness in spontaneous, carefree moments.

How can you embrace the unpredictability of life, allowing yourself to truly unwind and enjoy the present?

"You can't hold back the moon, can't stop the ebb and flow.
The water still comes, and the water still goes."

Slack Tide (2020)

Life's natural rhythms can't be controlled—just like you can't hold back the moon or stop the tides from ebbing and flowing. This sentiment encourages you to relax and go with the flow, accepting that change is a constant part of life.

Embrace the tranquility of letting things be, and find joy in the present moment. How can you let go of control and unwind, enjoying the ebb and flow of life as it comes?

"I gotta second story view from curb to curb; I gotta sign that reads 'Do Not Disturb.' A monogrammed towel and a bucket of ice. A chest of drawers and a mirror that lies."

This Hotel Room (1976)

Sometimes, the best way to unwind is to find a quiet spot with a great view and a "Do Not Disturb" sign. The simple pleasures of life, like a cozy room, a cold drink, and a bit of peace and quiet, create the perfect setting for relaxation. Take a break from the hustle and bustle to enjoy moments of stillness and simplicity.

How can you carve out time in your busy life to fully relax and recharge, savoring the small comforts that bring you joy?

"Down to the banana republics, down to the tropical sun go the expatriated Americans hopin' to find some fun. Some of them go for the sailing, called by the lure of the sea tryin' to find what is ailing living in the land of the free."

Banana Republics (1977)

Sometimes, the allure of tropical sun and adventure calls out, drawing people away from their usual routines in search of fun and new experiences. Whether it's the lure of the sea or the desire for a different pace of life, many embark on journeys hoping to find what's missing in their lives. This sentiment reflects the universal quest for fulfillment and the healing power of exploration.

How can you embrace the spirit of adventure and seek out experiences that bring you joy and satisfaction, wherever they may be?

"Oh, Mexico. It sounds so sweet with the sun sinkin' low.
The moon so bright likes to light up the night, make everything alright."

Mexico (1995)

Oh, Mexico. The allure of its sweet, sun-soaked evenings and bright, moonlit nights promises a sense of tranquility and escape. As the sun sinks low and the moon lights up the night, everything seems to fall into place, making the world feel alright.

This sentiment captures the essence of finding peace and relaxation in a beautiful, faraway place. How can you embrace these moments of serenity and let the magic of such places wash away your worries?

A Pirate Looks at Forty

Life's journey is a tapestry woven with adventures, memories, and a touch of nostalgia. Inspired by Jimmy Buffett's reflective and adventurous spirit, this chapter explores the richness of past experiences and the wisdom they bring.

These quotes delve into the thrill of risky endeavors, the resilience born from challenges, and the bittersweet beauty of looking back. Embrace the stories that shape you, the lessons learned from daring to live boldly, and the appreciation of life's highs and lows. Let these reflections guide you through the uncharted waters of your own adventures and the reflections they inspire.

"I've done a bit of smugglin', and I've run my share of grass. I made enough money to buy Miami, but I pissed it away so fast. Never meant to last, never meant to last."

A Pirate Looks at Forty (1974)

Buffett's words capture the thrill of risky endeavors and the ease with which success can slip through our fingers. The lyric reminds us that the material gains we chase are often temporary, and the true value lies in the experiences and stories we gather along the way. His candid acknowledgment of squandered riches speaks to the human tendency to seek excitement and the inevitable ups and downs that come with it.

Ultimately, Buffett's lyric is a celebration of living boldly and accepting the transient nature of life's highs and lows. It encourages us to embrace our past with a sense of humor and to recognize that not all things are meant to last. In doing so, we find freedom in the present moment and appreciation for the adventures that shape our journey.

"I've proved who I am so many times the magnetic strip's worn thin.
And each time I was someone else, and everyone was taken in."

Pacing The Cage (1999)

This lyric captures the exhaustion of constantly reinventing one-self to meet the expectations of others. The image of a worn-out magnetic strip symbolizes the toll taken by repeatedly proving one's identity, while the experience of being different people to different audiences highlights the pressures of conforming.

Consider the times you've had to adapt or change to fit into various roles or environments. How has this affected your sense of self? Today, reflect on the importance of authenticity and the courage it takes to be true to who you are. Embrace the idea that you don't need to prove yourself to anyone. Instead, focus on nurturing your true identity and finding environments where you can thrive as your genuine self. This reminder encourages us to value our own worth and to seek connections that accept us for who we truly are.

"I've been treated well. I raised all kinds of hell when a full tank
was only a fin. Ain't it quite funny how things turn around?"

I Heard I Was in Town (1982)

This lyric reflects on the nostalgia and the passage of time,
highlighting how much things can change. From carefree
days of raising hell to more reflective moments, it's a re-
minder of how life evolves in unexpected ways.

Reflect on your own journey and the changes you've seen
over the years. What are the moments that stand out, both
wild and tame? How have you grown and adapted to life's
twists and turns? Today, appreciate the journey you've
been on and recognize the humor and wisdom that come
with looking back. Life has a way of turning around, often
in surprising and wonderful ways.

"Do I lie like a loungeroom lizard? Or do I sing like a bird released?"

Weather with You (2006)

Life often presents us with a choice: to stay comfortable and stagnant or to embrace freedom and express ourselves fully. This lyric captures the tension between complacency and the exhilarating feeling of liberation.

Reflect on moments when you've had to choose between staying in your comfort zone and taking a leap of faith. How did those choices impact your life? Today, consider where you might be holding back and how you can embrace the freedom to truly be yourself. Whether it's pursuing a passion or speaking your truth, choose to sing like a bird released, and experience the joy that comes with it.

"We never knew anything groovy. A dime meant bread and not a movie. The muscles that controlled my smile were rarely ever used, 'cause there's nothing soft about hard times."

There's Nothin' Soft About Hard Times (1970)

Hard times often leave little room for joy, making even the simplest pleasures seem out of reach. This lyric captures the struggle of living through tough periods when survival takes precedence over happiness. It's a stark reminder of the resilience required to endure such times.

Reflect on your own experiences with hardship and how they shaped you. How did you find moments of strength and perseverance?

Acknowledge the difficulty of those times but also recognize the resilience you've developed. Embrace the small victories and moments of joy that you can now appreciate, knowing that they are hard-earned. Remember, even in tough times, the human spirit can find ways to endure and thrive.

"And when I get older and I have a daughter, I'll teach her to sing, and play her my song. And I'll tell her some stories I can barely remember and hope that she will sing along."

Something So Feminine About a Mandolin (1976)

Passing down traditions and stories creates a bridge between generations. This lyric beautifully captures the desire to share our experiences, songs, and memories with those we love, hoping they'll find joy and meaning in them too.

Reflect on the stories and traditions that have been passed down to you. How have they shaped who you are?

Think about what you'd like to share with future generations. Whether it's a song, a story, or a cherished memory, these connections keep our heritage alive and create lasting bonds. Embrace the joy of teaching and sharing, knowing it keeps the spirit of those moments alive.

"That's my story and I'm sticking to it. That's my life and all that I got. Call me a liar, call me a writer, believe me or not."

That's My Story and I'm Sticking to It (1989)

The stories we tell ourselves and others are powerful, even if they aren't always aligned with reality. This lyric highlights the importance of embracing our personal narratives, acknowledging that sometimes our truths are subjective. It's a reminder that our perception shapes our reality.

Reflect on the stories you tell about your life. Are they based on reality, or are they shaped by your experiences and emotions? Today, consider the impact of these narratives on your sense of self. Embrace your story with an open mind, recognizing that while it may not always align with objective reality, it holds significant personal truth and meaning.

"You're one of our own down there. You'll never drink alone down there. Good god, I feel at home down there."

Bama Breeze (2006)

Finding a place where you truly belong is a priceless treasure. This lyric celebrates the warmth and camaraderie of a community that welcomes you as one of their own. It's about the comfort and joy of being surrounded by people who make you feel at home.

Reflect on the places and people that give you that deep sense of belonging. What makes you feel truly at home? Today, cherish those connections and think about how you can create that welcoming environment for others. Remember, community and companionship are the heartbeats that make any place feel like home.

"Oh, that summer sun, wind in your hair—
half the fun is getting there."

The Slow Lane (2020)

Life's journey is often as enjoyable as the destination itself. This lyric celebrates the simple pleasures of a summer day and the joy of the adventure. It's a reminder to savor the moments along the way and to find happiness in the journey, not just the arrival.

Reflect on your own travels and adventures. How have the experiences along the way added to your enjoyment? Today, focus on the process rather than the outcome. Embrace the wind in your hair and the warmth of the sun, finding joy in each step of your journey. Remember, half the fun is getting there.

"And if this all blows up and goes to hell, I can still see us sittin' on the bed in some motel listenin' to the stories we could tell."

Stories We Could Tell (1974)

Even when everything seems to be falling apart, there's solace in cherished memories and shared experiences. This quote speaks to the enduring power of intimate moments and personal stories that bind us together, even in tough times. It reminds us that no matter how chaotic life gets, the simple, heartfelt connections we make with others remain a source of comfort and strength.

Reflect on a moment with a loved one that brings you peace and joy. How can these treasured memories help you navigate through challenging times?

"I got my Hush Puppies on;
I guess I never was meant for glitter rock 'n' roll."

Come Monday (1974)

Embracing your true self means recognizing where you fit and where you don't. This lyric speaks to the comfort of staying true to your identity, even if it means steering clear of the flashier paths others might take. It's a reminder that authenticity often brings the most peace.

Reflect on the areas of your life where you've felt pressure to conform. How can you embrace your own style and preferences more fully? Today, celebrate what makes you uniquely you. Whether it's a pair of comfortable shoes or a preference for simpler pleasures, honoring your true self will always lead to greater contentment.

"It's a semi-true story, believe it or not. I made up a few things and there's some I forgot, but the life and the telling are both real to me."

Semi-True Story (1999)

Sometimes, stories are a mix of truth and embellishment, where some details are invented and others forgotten. Yet, the essence of the life lived and the tales told remain authentic. These moments blend together, forming a narrative that is both real and imagined.

This perspective highlights how our memories and stories shape our understanding of life. How can you appreciate the blend of fact and fiction in your own experiences, recognizing the richness they add to your personal history? The beauty lies in conveying deeper truths through this unique mix, enriching your journey and understanding.

"As a dreamer of dreams and a travelin' man, I have chalked up many
a mile. Read dozens of books about heroes and crooks,
and I learned much from both of their styles."

Son of a Son of a Sailor (1978)

Dreamers and travelers gather wisdom from every journey and
story. With many miles behind and countless adventures ahead,
there's a wealth of knowledge in the tales of heroes and crooks
alike. Each has a lesson, shaping our perspectives and enriching
our lives.

Embrace the diversity of experiences, and remember that wis-
dom comes from all walks of life, both virtuous and flawed. How
have the stories you've encountered and the paths you've traveled
shaped who you are today?

"It's three o'clock in the morning, running on adrenalin.
What I'm trying to say is that tomorrow's the day,
and we've got to do it over again."

Kick It in Second Wind (1976)

The exhilaration of late-night moments, fueled by adrenaline, captures the essence of life's relentless pace. At three in the morning, when the world is quiet (or getting there), there's a unique clarity about the urgency of tomorrow's tasks and the cycle of daily routines. These moments highlight the persistence and resilience required to tackle each new day, even when we're running on empty. It's a reminder that life is a series of ongoing challenges and opportunities, where our determination and drive play crucial roles.

Embrace the push that keeps you going and find strength in knowing that each dawn brings a fresh start. How do you stay motivated and ready to face the new challenges of tomorrow, even when it feels like you're just catching your breath?

"Then the glitz and all the glamour hit like a hurricane
or maybe we just all grew up, but it never was the same."

Autour Du Rocher (2002)

The transformative impact of sudden change can hit like a
hurricane, bringing with it a whirlwind of glitz and glamour.
Whether it's a significant event or simply the passage of time,
these moments can irrevocably alter our experiences and
perceptions. There's a sense of nostalgia for how things used
to be, reminding us that life is constantly evolving. Adapting
to new realities while cherishing past memories is essential.

Reflect on how sudden changes or the process of growing up
have shaped your journey and altered your perspective on
life. How do you balance embracing the new with holding
onto the cherished moments of the past?

"It's time to see the world. It's time to kiss a girl. It's time to cross the wild meridian. Grab your bag and take a chance. Time to learn a cajun dance. Kid your gonna see the mornin' sun."

The Pascagoula Run (1989)

Embracing the call to adventure, this sentiment captures the excitement of new beginnings and the thrill of exploration. It's about seizing the moment to see the world, take risks, and experience life's vibrant tapestry—from kissing a girl to learning a Cajun dance. Crossing the wild meridian signifies stepping into the unknown with a sense of wonder and courage.

This quote reminds us that change and transition are opportunities for growth and joy. How can you embrace life's adventures and transitions, maintaining a sense of humor and perspective as you embark on new journeys?

"'Jambalaya' was the only song I could sing. Chasin' after sparrows
with rubber-tip arrows, knowin' I could never hurt a thing.
Life was just a tire swing ."

Life is Just a Tire Swing (1974)

Reflecting on the innocence and simplicity of childhood, this
sentiment paints a nostalgic picture of carefree days. The smell
of the creosote plant, Easter meals with quirky relatives, and
the winds blowing across the bayou evoke a tranquil, bygone
era. Childhood memories of swinging on a tire, singing "Jam-
balaya," picking blackberries, and eating fried chicken encap-
sulate a time untouched by pain. Life's simplicity extended to
summer camps and daydreams inspired by an RCA Victrola.
Even after surviving a close call on an Illinois road, the essence
of those carefree days remains.

How can you reconnect with the innocence and simplicity of
your own past, finding joy and solace in the small, carefree
moments of life?

"We are the people, there isn't any doubt.
We are the people they still can't figure out."

We Are the People Our Parents Warned Us About (1983)

Embracing the spirit of individuality and resilience, this sentiment highlights the enigmatic nature of those who live life on their own terms. Despite being hard to figure out, they remain unapologetically unique, reflecting on a life filled with adventures and memories. It's a celebration of those who carve their own path and leave a lasting impression.

How can you embrace your own uniqueness and cherish the adventures that define your life, even when others can't quite understand your journey?

"With no plans for the future, he still seems in control.
From a bronco ride to a ten-foot tide, he just had to learn to roll."

Cowboy in the Jungle (1978)

Reflecting on the adventures and lessons of life, this sentiment captures the spirit of adaptability and resilience. With no fixed plans for the future, he manages to stay in control by learning to roll with whatever comes his way. Whether it's a bronco ride or a ten-foot tide, facing life's challenges with flexibility and courage is key.

This approach to life embodies the essence of a journey filled with unexpected twists and turns. How can you embrace a resilient and adaptable mindset, drawing strength from your past experiences to navigate the future?

"We're all somewhere over China, headin' east or headin' west. Takin' time to live a little, flying so far from the nest just to put a little distance between causes and effects, like an ancient fortune teller knowin' who and what comes next."

Somewhere Over China (1982)

Embracing the spirit of adventure and reflection, this sentiment captures the essence of exploring new horizons and gaining wisdom along the way. Traveling far from the nest, whether heading east or west, offers a chance to live fully and understand life's complexities. Like an ancient fortune teller anticipating what comes next, this journey creates distance between causes and effects, providing clarity and insight.

How can you continue to seek new experiences and adventures, using them to reflect on your past and shape your future?

"I guess every good picker has had some hard times;
I sure had my share. It's really kinda funny to laugh at 'em now,
but I don't want to go back there."

Peanut Butter Conspiracy (1973)

Reflecting on the hard times faced along the journey. While these tough moments are now a source of humor, there's a clear recognition of not wanting to return to those challenging times. This perspective highlights the growth and resilience gained from overcoming adversity.

How can you appreciate the lessons learned from your past struggles while focusing on the positive direction your life is now heading?

"Years grow shorter, not longer, the more you've been on your own. Feelin's for movin' grow stronger, so you wonder why you ever go home."

Wonder Why We Ever Go Home (1977)

Reflecting on the passage of time and the increasing desire for adventure, this sentiment captures the bittersweet realization that years seem to grow shorter the longer you've been on your own. As the urge to keep moving intensifies, you begin to question the idea of ever returning home. This perspective speaks to the wanderer's spirit and the pull of the unknown, highlighting the tension between stability and the call of the open road.

How can you balance the longing for adventure with the comfort of home, finding fulfillment in both?

"I remember as a child all the happiness and smiles that flowed around my grandma's Sunday table. While Auntie Mae was sayin' grace, Papa T would sneak a taste and catch a funny look from my cousin Mabel."

Creola (1986)

Reminiscing about childhood memories, this sentiment captures the warmth and joy that filled grandma's Sunday table. The happiness and smiles shared among family members create a nostalgic scene of togetherness. Auntie Mae saying grace while Papa T sneaks a taste and catches a funny look from cousin Mabel reflects the playful and loving dynamics of family gatherings.

These moments highlight the cherished simplicity and affection that define our fondest memories. How can you hold onto these precious memories and create similar moments of joy and connection in your own life?

"Look in the mirror, and what do I see—
the gypsy and fool that I always will be."

Everybody's on the Run (1985)

Reflecting on one's identity, this sentiment captures the essence of self-awareness and acceptance. Looking in the mirror reveals a gypsy spirit and a fool, acknowledging the wandering, adventurous nature alongside moments of folly. It's an honest embrace of one's true self, recognizing the blend of wisdom and whimsy that defines a life well-lived.

How can you accept and celebrate the unique aspects of your own identity, finding strength in both your adventures and your mistakes?

"I'm turning off the waterfall the tourists can go home. I feel it time to travel take time to write a poem. Time to seek some therapy; I'm going walkabout. Answers are the easy part, questions raise the doubt."

Off to See the Lizard (1989)

Embracing the need for reflection and a change of pace, this sentiment captures the desire to step back from the familiar and delve into self-discovery. Turning off the waterfall and allowing the tourists to go home symbolizes a retreat from the hustle and bustle. It's a time to travel, write poetry, and seek therapy, embarking on a personal walkabout.

This journey is about finding clarity and understanding that while answers might be straightforward, it's the questions that provoke deeper thought and doubt. How can you take time to explore and reflect, seeking wisdom in the journey and the questions it raises?

"If he'd only known how the years would fly on by.
Such a simple crime, he's run out of time, so he reaches for the sky."

Frenchman for the Night (1994)

Reflecting on the swift passage of time, this sentiment captures the bittersweet realization of missed opportunities. If only he'd known how quickly the years would fly by, he might have lived differently. Now, facing the end of his journey, he reaches for the sky, striving to make the most of the time he has left.

This perspective serves as a poignant reminder to cherish every moment and live fully, before time runs out. How can you seize the present and make the most of your days, ensuring you live without regrets?

Fins, Flames, and Family

"Relationships! We all got 'em. We all want 'em!
What do we do with them?"
—Jimmy Buffett

Connections with others add depth and color to our lives. This section dives into the complexities and joys of human connection. Whether it's the comfort of a steadfast friend, the lessons from past loves, or the bond with kindred spirits, these quotes remind us of the importance of companionship.

Explore the reflections on love, loyalty, and the bittersweet moments that define our relationships. Let these insights encourage you to cherish the people in your life and the connections that make your journey meaningful.

"Can't you feel them circling, honey? Can't you feel them swimming
around? You got fins to the left, fins to the right,
and you're the only bait in town."

Fins (1979)

There's a thrill in feeling the world swirl around you, espe-
cially when you find yourself the center of attention. This
vivid imagery of fins circling captures the excitement and
tension of being in the spotlight. It's a playful reminder of
those moments when all eyes are on you, and you're navi-
gating the lively currents of social interaction.

Embrace the energy and let it remind you of your own
charisma and allure. Whether it's in the midst of a bustling
crowd or during a lively gathering, relish in being the life
of the party. How do you handle the exhilaration of being
the center of attention?

"No interruptions from the telephone. Dont need call waitin', just you and me alone."

Six String Music (1994)

In a world filled with constant distractions, finding uninterrupted time with loved ones is a precious gift. This lyric reminds us of the importance of disconnecting from technology to fully connect with each other.

Reflect on the last time you shared a moment free from digital interruptions. How did it impact your connection? Today, make a conscious effort to carve out distraction-free time with someone special. Turn off the phone, forget about call waiting, and focus on the joy of being fully present with each other. True connection happens when we give our undivided attention.

"Talk and talk and talk until your jaws turn blue, but you never really tell me what you're gonna do. Seem to keep it all locked up inside, I can't help but start to thinkin' you've got somethin' to hide."

Lip Service (1982)

Some conversations seem endless, yet leave us with more questions than answers. This lyric captures the frustration of hearing words without action, and the suspicion that comes with secrets kept locked away.

Reflect on the relationships in your life. How often do you find yourself talking in circles, without real communication or resolution? Today, focus on being open and honest in your interactions. Share your intentions clearly and encourage others to do the same.

Strive for meaningful conversations that foster connection and clarity. By breaking down barriers and expressing yourself openly, you can create deeper, more trusting relationships and dispel any lingering doubts or suspicions.

"Ohhh, these moments we're left with, may you always remember these moments are shared by few."

Lovely Cruise (1977)

Moments shared with loved ones are fleeting yet precious, highlighting the rarity and significance of these special times. It's important to cherish the time spent with those close to us, recognizing how meaningful these shared experiences are.

Reflect on the significant moments in your life and the people with whom you've shared them. How have these experiences shaped your relationships and memories?

Take a moment to appreciate and honor those connections. Reach out to those who have been part of your cherished memories and let them know how much they mean to you. By valuing and remembering these times, you ensure they continue to hold a special place in your heart.

"I think that I might die if I miss anything at all.
Text me, send me an e-mail, ring me up, give me a call!"

Everybody's on the Phone (2006)

In our hyper-connected world, the fear of missing out (FOMO) can be overwhelming. This lyric humorously captures the anxiety of staying in the loop and the constant need for communication. It's a reminder to balance our digital lives with real, meaningful connections.

Reflect on your own relationship with technology and communication. Are you truly connecting or just keeping up? Today, focus on fostering genuine interactions rather than just staying updated. Reach out to someone in a meaningful way, and remember that while staying informed is important, authentic connections are what truly enrich our lives.

"What a fool I have been. There's no way I can win
unless you take me back in."

When the Wild Life Betrays Me (1984)

Admitting our mistakes is never easy, but it's a crucial step toward healing and reconciliation. This lyric speaks to the vulnerability and humility required to seek forgiveness and the hope for a second chance. It's a reminder that growth often comes from acknowledging our errors and making amends.

Reflect on a time when you realized you were in the wrong. How did you seek to make things right? Today, embrace the courage it takes to admit your mistakes and ask for forgiveness. Remember, true strength lies in recognizing our flaws and striving to mend what's broken. Seek the grace to be let back in and the wisdom to learn from your missteps.

"And I miss you so badly, well, I love you madly. Feelin' so sad now since I been gone, gone, gone. And it gets quite confusin', it seems that I'm losin' track of the long days since I been home."

Miss You So Badly (1977)

The ache of missing someone deeply and the longing to be re-united is powerfully expressed in this sentiment. It captures the intensity of love and the sadness that comes with separation. Feeling confused and losing track of time emphasize the emotional turmoil experienced when away from a loved one.

This quote highlights the profound impact that relationships and connections have on our hearts and minds. How can you cherish and strengthen the bonds with those you love, ensuring that distance and time apart only deepen your connection?

"My love is guaranteed. You're never going to see the end of me. I've got all you need."

Money Back Guarantee (1992)

Just like a money-back guarantee, true love comes with a promise of unwavering support and endless presence. This love ensures you'll never see the end of it, providing all you need without fail. It reflects the strength and reliability that form the foundation of deep, enduring relationships.

How can you nurture and appreciate the steadfast love in your life, ensuring that it remains a constant source of support and fulfillment?

"Hard to believe it's happening, but my whole world's
shrunken to all the ways I want you."

All the Ways I Want You (2002)

It's hard to believe, but sometimes your whole world can
shrink down to all the ways you desire and need someone.
This sentiment captures the intense focus and longing that
true love brings, where nothing else seems to matter as
much as the connection you share. The feeling of your
entire universe revolving around one person highlights the
depth and intensity of this bond.

How can you embrace and cherish this powerful emotion,
ensuring that it deepens and enriches your relationships,
making them even more fulfilling and meaningful? By
nurturing this connection, you can create a lasting and
profound love that stands the test of time.

"When I'm holding you tight, you give me the power
to burn like a torch in the darkest hour."

Anything, Anytime, Anywhere (2004)

In the moments of holding someone tight, they provide the strength and power to shine brightly, even in the darkest times. This connection ignites a torch within, offering warmth and light when it's needed most. The bond you share becomes a source of resilience and courage, illuminating the path ahead.

How can you nurture this empowering connection, ensuring that it continues to provide strength and comfort during life's challenging moments? By valuing and deepening this bond, you can create a source of enduring support and inspiration.

"Your wholesale price is much to high to pay.
A bargain counter atmosphere is no way to sell love, a
nd I can't be your blessing from above."

I Can' Be Your Hero Today (1970)

In matters of love, authenticity and sincerity are priceless. This sentiment speaks to the idea that true love cannot be bought or sold at a bargain. It's a reminder that genuine relationships require mutual respect and genuine effort, far beyond any superficial transactions. Trying to sell love cheaply, in a bargain counter atmosphere, undermines its true value and significance.

Love should be a blessing, a profound connection, not something commodified. Reflect on how you approach relationships and ensure that they are built on a foundation of genuine affection and mutual respect. How can you cultivate and cherish the true value of love in your life?

"As large as life, she stood there, kissed my cheek and called my old nickname. And though several years had passed, both of us still looked quite the same."

Turnabout (1970)

Sometimes, life brings unexpected reunions that transport us back in time. Seeing a familiar face after years, feeling the warmth of a kiss on the cheek, and hearing an old nickname can evoke powerful memories. Despite the passage of time, some connections remain unchanged, reminding us of the enduring bonds that shape our lives. These moments highlight the beauty of lasting relationships and the comfort of familiarity.

Reflect on the cherished connections in your life and the joy they bring when rekindled. How can you nurture these bonds and appreciate the timelessness of genuine relationships?

"This comes from deep in my soul. Your sweet love has taken control. I'll swim across the ocean if you tell me so. Take you to the jump up if you want to go. It's never too late to make a brand new start."

Knees of My Heart (1984)

Love has a profound way of inspiring us to make grand gestures and embrace new beginnings. When love takes control deep in your soul, it drives you to cross oceans and embark on adventures for the one you cherish. This sentiment captures the boundless energy and commitment that love can bring, reminding us that it's never too late to start anew.

Embrace the power of love to fuel your passion and take bold steps towards creating fresh, meaningful experiences. How can you harness the strength of love to make a brand new start and pursue the dreams that matter most to you?

"Sometimes I catch her dreamin' and wonder where that little mind meanders. Is she strollin' along the shore or cruisin' over the broad savannah? I know someday she'll learn to make up her own rhymes. Someday she's gonna learn how to fly. Oh, that I won't deny."

Little Miss Magic (1981)

Reflecting on the dreams and future of a child captures the essence of love and the deep connections we make. Watching a little one dream and grow, imagining where their mind wanders—be it along a shore or over a savannah—speaks to the boundless potential within them. This sentiment embraces the beauty of nurturing and witnessing a child's journey as they learn, create, and eventually spread their wings to fly.

It's a reminder of the precious bond and the joy of seeing someone you love grow into their own. How can you cherish and support the dreams of those you hold dear, encouraging them to reach their fullest potential?

"Tried to phone from Paris thinking things could be arranged.
Me and you would rendezvous but I found your number changed,
so I drove to San Remo where the crazy painter dwells.
Toasted our old photograph still up there on his shelf."

Distantly in Love (1983)

This nostalgic journey highlights the twists and turns of life and
the attempts to reconnect with the past. Trying to arrange a
rendezvous from Paris only to find a number changed, and then
driving to San Remo to visit an old friend, captures the bitter-
sweet nature of memories and lost connections. Toasting an old
photograph on a painter's shelf reflects the sentimental value of
cherished moments and the lessons learned from them.

This quote encourages introspection and appreciating the paths
we've taken. How do your own journeys and memories shape
your present and guide your personal growth?

"So tell me all your troubles, I'll surely tell you mine.
We'll laugh and smoke and cuss and joke and have a glass of wine."

When the Coast is Clear (1986)

The essence of connection and camaraderie shines through in the simple act of sharing troubles and joys with a friend. Laughing, smoking, cussing, and joking over a glass of wine captures the spirit of genuine companionship.

These moments remind us that the bonds we form with others, through honest conversation and shared experiences, bring comfort and joy. It's about finding solace and happiness in each other's company, no matter what life throws your way.

How can you nurture the relationships that bring laughter, support, and a sense of belonging into your life?

"And I got presents to send you. Even got money to lend you. But honey I could never ever pretend your not there on my mind."

Presents to Send You (1974)

Expressing the depth of affection and constant thoughts of a loved one, this sentiment emphasizes genuine connection. Despite having presents to send and money to lend, nothing compares to the unwavering presence of someone special on your mind. It's a reminder that true love and care go beyond material gestures, residing in the constant thoughts and emotions shared with another.

How can you nurture and express the deep connections you have, ensuring your loved ones know they are always in your thoughts?

"We both done our share of runnin' around, so we know enough to know the kind of love we've found. It's the real thing, and we've got to see it through."

Burn That Bridge (1984)

This sentiment speaks to the wisdom gained from past experiences and the deep appreciation for a genuine, enduring love. After years of running around, the realization of finding the real thing brings a sense of commitment and determination to see it through. It's a celebration of mature love, built on understanding and shared experiences.

How can you cherish and nurture the profound connections in your life, ensuring they flourish and endure?

"I've had good days and bad days and going half mad days.
I try to let go, but you're still on my mind. I've lost all the old ways;
I'm searching for new plays. Putting it all on the line."

If the Phone Doesn't Ring, It's Me (1985)

Navigating through the ups and downs of life, this sentiment captures the struggle of trying to move on while still being haunted by memories of someone special. The mix of good days, bad days, and moments of madness highlights the emotional journey.

Letting go of the past and searching for new ways forward reflects a bold commitment to growth and transformation. It's about putting everything on the line to find a new path. How can you embrace change and seek new opportunities while honoring the emotions that linger from the past?

"Well stories have endings and fantasies fade. The guard by the door starts drawing the shade, so write your own ending and hope they come true for the lovers and strangers on Bay Avenue."

Love in the Library (1994)

As chapters close and dreams evolve, there's a beauty in crafting your own love story. Even when moments seem to fade, the power to create new beginnings and lasting connections remains. This sentiment encourages you to cherish the relationships and encounters that shape your journey.

For those fleeting loves and chance meetings, it's a reminder to infuse your story with hope and intention. How can you write your own romantic narrative, filled with meaningful moments and enduring connections?

"These days I'm up about the time I used to go to bed. Living large was once the deal, now I watch the stars instead. They are timeless and predictable unlike most things that I do; but I tell the wind and my old friend I'm headed home to you."

Coast of Carolina (2004)

Reflecting on the shift from a life of late nights and extravagance to one of quiet contemplation, this sentiment captures the wisdom that comes with age. Trading the thrill of living large for the serenity of watching the stars, there's a newfound appreciation for the timeless and predictable. Amidst life's uncertainties, the comfort of old friends and the promise of returning home bring a sense of peace.

This perspective highlights the importance of family and enduring connections. How can you find balance between the excitement of the past and the tranquility of the present, cherishing the constants that guide you home to loved ones?

"In the roll of cosmic dice, you win one heart and lose it twice before you know. Love is fine until you taste this melancholy bouillabaisse called letting go."

Lage Nom Ai (1995)

In the unpredictable game of life, the highs and lows of love can be intense. You might find and lose love more than once, tasting both the sweetness of connection and the bittersweet challenge of letting go. This sentiment captures the emotional rollercoaster of relationships, highlighting the strength needed to navigate these profound experiences.

How can you embrace both the joys and sorrows of love, finding resilience and wisdom along the way?

"And some of the things I've seen, maybe she won't have to see.
But there's a lot I want to pass along that was handed down to me."

Delaney Talks to Statues (1994)

Reflecting on life's experiences, there's a hope that the next generation might avoid certain hardships. Yet, there's a wealth of wisdom and lessons worth passing down, treasures inherited from those who came before. There's a strong desire to protect loved ones while sharing valuable insights and traditions.

How can you ensure that the wisdom you've gained is passed along, enriching the lives of those who follow?

"I can't fax you my love; I can't e-mail my heart; I can't see your face in cyberspace; I don't know where to start. I'm light years behind, from the age they call stone; I'm a carbon-based caveman, honey, just flesh and bone."

Flesh and Bone (1999)

In a world dominated by technology, expressing true emotions can feel challenging. Love can't be faxed, hearts can't be emailed, and faces are lost in cyberspace. Feeling light years behind in this digital age, there's a longing for genuine, human connection.

This sentiment emphasizes the simplicity and authenticity of being a "carbon-based caveman," just flesh and bone, seeking real interaction. How can you prioritize heartfelt, tangible connections in a world that increasingly relies on digital communication?

"Cameron's contemplating; I'm not sure just what he thinks. 'Is my dad some kind of lunatic with his stories and hijinks?' Then he says when I get old and gray and feel like I'm marooned, he will take me in his rocket ship to that beach house on the moon."

Beach House on the Moon (1999)

Jimmy's son might be pondering whether his dad's stories and antics are a bit over the top, but there's a heartwarming promise beneath the humor. Imagining a future where, even when feeling marooned in old age, a rocket ship ride to a beach house on the moon is a testament to the bond they share. This sentiment highlights the love and commitment within family, promising to care for each other through life's adventures and uncertainties.

How can you nurture and cherish the bonds with your loved ones, ensuring they know you'll always be there for them, no matter what?

"Maybe I can parlez a little Francais. Maybe I can even write a whole page a day. Do a crossword puzzle in a minute or two, but I learned to be cool from you."

We Learned to Be Cool From You (2009)

Achievements like speaking French, writing prolifically, or solving crossword puzzles quickly are impressive, but the coolest lessons often come from those we admire. This sentiment highlights the influence of loved ones in teaching us to stay calm, composed, and genuinely cool. It's a reminder that while skills and talents are valuable, the wisdom and demeanor we gain from important people in our lives are truly priceless.

How can you honor and share the cool, composed qualities you've learned from those who inspire you?

"There's other situations that might challenge you I guess. When your daughter tries out for the football team and your son tries on her dress. And you start to think that the devil's in charge of how you're situated. Life is still worth living it's just simply complicated."

Simply Complicated (2004)

Family life is full of unexpected challenges and surprises that test our understanding and patience. When faced with situations like a daughter trying out for the football team or a son experimenting with different identities, it can feel overwhelming. Yet, these moments are part of the rich tapestry of family and interpersonal relationships. Life's complexities and unconventional twists make it uniquely beautiful and worth living. This sentiment encourages embracing the unpredictability of family dynamics with humor and resilience.

How can you navigate the intricate web of relationships, finding joy and strength in the diverse experiences that shape your family life?

"All those little things that my grandfather said, not so little now, here in my grown-up head. I didn't always see the wisdom at the time, but I'm older now."

Equal Strain on All Parts (2023)

The seemingly small pieces of advice and wisdom from your grandfather take on new significance as you grow older. What once seemed trivial now resonates deeply in your adult life. These words, which may have been overlooked in youth, now shine with clarity and importance. This sentiment reflects on the value of generational wisdom and how its importance becomes clearer over time. As you navigate life's challenges and joys, these lessons become guiding principles.

How can you honor and reflect on the wisdom passed down to you, appreciating its impact on your life as you grow and evolve?

It's five O'Clock Somewhere

There's a special kind of magic in letting go and embracing the present moment. This section is inspired by the carefree philosophy that celebrates the joy of living in the now.

Through these quotes, we explore the importance of taking breaks, finding moments of fun, and letting loose from life's pressures. Whether it's enjoying a spontaneous adventure, indulging in a little mischief, or simply relaxing with a drink in hand, these reflections remind us that it's okay to pause and savor the moment. Embrace the freedom and joy that comes from living as if it's always five o'clock somewhere.

"At a moment like this, I can't help but wonder,
what would Jimmy Buffet do?"

It's Five O'Clock Somewhere (2003)

Although this line is typically delivered by Alan Jackson or
Mac McAnally, this tune has become a staple for Parrot-
heads across the globe. In moments of uncertainty or re-
laxation, channeling the spirit of Jimmy Buffett can bring a
sense of ease and joy. Embrace a carefree, laid-back attitude,
and find pleasure in the simple things. Whether it's enjoying
a tropical drink, soaking up the sun, or taking a break from
the hustle, adopting Jimmy's relaxed approach can make any
moment brighter.

How can you incorporate this laid-back mindset into your
life, savoring the present and finding happiness in the here
and now?

"And now I must confess, I could use some rest. I can't run at this pace very long. Yes, it's quite insane. I think it hurts my brain. But it cleans me out then I can go on."

Trying to Reason With Hurricane Season (1974)

Buffett's words capture the feeling of being overwhelmed by the relentless pace of life. We all reach points where we need to slow down and recharge. Pushing ourselves too hard can leave us feeling burnt out and frazzled, but taking a break can rejuvenate our spirits and clear our minds.

Reflect on a time when you felt exhausted and how taking a step back helped you regain your balance. What can you do today to give yourself the rest you need? Remember, it's okay to pause, recharge, and then continue with a clearer, stronger mindset.

"Well, it seems like I've run out of reasons to be here, so I'm just gonna steal from myself: if your attitude's appalling, there's a latitude that's calling. Get yourself past that continental shelf."

Party at the End of the World (2006)

The world is filled with turmoil and absurdities, yet amidst the chaos, there's the promise of a grand escape—a party at the end of the world, where worries can be left behind and joy can be found in the moment.

The message is clear: when your current situation feels unbearable and your attitude needs a shift, sometimes the best remedy is to change your latitude. By moving beyond familiar boundaries, you can find a renewed sense of freedom and joy. Embrace the adventure of seeking new places and experiences, rediscovering our zest for life. How can you create opportunities for escape and renewal, even if it's just a small change in your routine? Embrace the adventure of exploring new horizons, and let the promise of new experiences lift your spirits.

"Well, now that's just the start of a well-deserved overdue binge. Meanwhile, back in the city, certain people are starting to cringe. His lawyers are calling his parents; his girlfriend doesn't know what to think; his partners are studying their options. He's just singing and ordering drinks!"

The Weather is Here, Wish You Were Beautiful (1981)

Sometimes, life calls for a well-deserved break from the grind, even if it causes a stir back in the city. While certain people cringe and worry, and his partners and loved ones scramble to make sense of his actions, he's reveling in the freedom of the moment. Singing and ordering drinks, he embodies the spirit of letting go and embracing joy, regardless of the consequences. This story highlights the importance of taking time for oneself and finding happiness, even amidst chaos.

How can you carve out moments to disconnect from pressures and indulge in the simple pleasures of life?

"Yeah, he loves livin' it up and takin' all of his time.
But he ain't givin' it up; it never crosses his mind."

Livin' It Up (1983)

Embracing a carefree lifestyle, the protagonist of this song relishes living life to the fullest and taking his time to enjoy every moment. The thought of giving up this joyous way of living never even crosses his mind. This sentiment celebrates the spirit of fully immersing oneself in the pleasures of life, refusing to succumb to the pressures of a hurried existence. It's a reminder to prioritize happiness and savor the experiences that bring joy and fulfillment.

How can you incorporate a similar sense of carefree enjoyment and steadfast commitment to happiness in your own life?

"Oh won't you take them to the carnival; let them play for hours. Tonight the weather feels so right; tomorrow feels like showers."

When Salome Plays the Drum (1982)

Embrace the joy of a carnival night, where the fun stretches for hours under perfect skies. This sentiment captures the magic of living in the moment, enjoying the present before the potential showers of tomorrow. It's a reminder to seize the day and find happiness in life's simple pleasures.

How can you fully savor the joyful moments and make the most of the present before they slip away?

"Pickup's washed and you just got paid, with any luck at all you might even get laid, 'cause they're pickin' and a kickin' on a Livingston Saturday night."

Livingston Saturday Night (1978)

Celebrating the carefree joy of a Saturday night, this scene captures the excitement of letting loose after a week of hard work. With a freshly washed pickup and a pocket full of pay, there's an air of possibility and adventure. The lively atmosphere of music and dancing embodies the spirit of living in the moment and enjoying life's simple pleasures.

It's a reminder to embrace the fun and spontaneity that weekends bring. How can you make the most of your downtime, savoring the thrill of carefree nights and joyful gatherings?

"It took a global crisis to remind us, there's so much more to life than workin' just a four-day week."

Nobody Works on Friday (2023)

While many cultures embrace extended periods of relaxation and celebration, the pressure to maintain productivity often keeps us tethered to our work. The French enjoy a month of joie de vivre, Aussies have their grilling weeks, Spain takes summer siestas, and Brazil heats up with bossa nova. A global health crisis reminded us that there's more to life than just working. It highlights the importance of flexibility and the need to prioritize relaxation and joy.

How can you incorporate more leisure and enjoyment into your routine, making sure you truly live and not just work?

"So, barmaid, bring a pitcher, another round of brew.
Honey, why don't we get drunk and screw?"

Why Don't We Get Drunk (And Screw) (1973)

Celebrating the carefree and unfiltered moments of life, this sentiment captures the essence of letting loose and living in the moment. Appreciating the company of a friend, even when things are a bit hazy, emphasizes the joy of spontaneous decisions. The light-hearted suggestion to get another round of drinks and have some fun highlights the spirit of embracing the present without overthinking.

How can you embrace spontaneity and enjoy the simple, unplanned moments that bring joy and laughter into your life?

"I love the now, all the pain and the pleasure. I love the now, all the blood and the treasure. It's the only circus that I know; it's the only ring where I'm allowed."

I Love the Now (1986)

Embracing the present moment with all its pain and pleasure, blood and treasure, this sentiment captures a deep appreciation for living in the now. Life is seen as a vibrant circus, where every experience, whether challenging or joyful, adds to the richness of the journey. It's a reminder to fully engage with the present and find joy and meaning in every moment.

How can you let go of worries about the past or future and fully embrace the here and now, making the most of every experience?

"Leave my cares behind. Take my own sweet time.
Ocean's on my mind."

Take Another Road (1989)

Embracing the spirit of relaxation and living in the moment, this sentiment captures the desire to leave cares behind and take life at a leisurely pace. With the ocean on your mind, it's about savoring the present and finding peace in the simplicity of life.

This perspective encourages you to slow down and enjoy the beauty around you, making the most of every moment. How can you adopt a more relaxed approach to life, letting go of stress and embracing the tranquility of the present?

"Come along let's have some fun, seems our work is done.
We'll barrel roll into the sun, just for starters."

Barometer Soup (1995)

Let's kick back and unwind now that the workday is over.
Picture yourself embarking on carefree adventures, soaking
up the sun, and relishing the thrill of living in the moment.

Life is about finding joy in the little things and embracing spon-
taneity whenever possible. How can you bring more laid-back
joy, spontaneous fun, and memorable experiences into your dai-
ly routine, ensuring you make the most of each moment?

"Hoping to catch a wave. Looking to misbehave,
as my lucky stars still shine above the sea."

Tides (2013)

Embracing the spirit of adventure and spontaneity, this sentiment captures the thrill of hoping to catch a wave and the playful desire to misbehave. With lucky stars shining above the sea, it's a reminder to live in the moment and enjoy life's simple pleasures. The excitement of the open water and the freedom to let loose create a perfect backdrop for unforgettable memories.

How can you seize the day, embracing fun and adventure while appreciating the magic that surrounds you and making the most of every moment?

"What if life is just a cosmic joke like spiders in your underwear or olives in your coke? My life can get as messy as a day-old sticky bun, so I arm myself with punch lines and a giant water gun."

What if the Hokey Pokey is All it Really is About? (2002)

Life often throws us unexpected surprises and can get quite messy, but facing it with a sense of humor makes it more enjoyable. Embracing a playful attitude and finding joy in the little things can make all the difference. Sometimes, simplifying our approach to life is the best way to navigate its complexities.

How about we take a break, relax with a cup of herbal tea, and appreciate the lighter side of life together?

"Time out, for bad behavior. Time off, you've been under the gun. High time somebody told you: it's time to let those puppies run."

Summerzcool (2009)

It's time for a well-deserved break from the pressures and stresses you've been under. You've been under the gun, and now it's time for a time out for bad behavior—a chance to let loose and enjoy life. This sentiment encourages you to take a step back, relax, and give yourself permission to unwind and have fun. High time someone reminded you to let those puppies run and embrace moments of freedom and joy.

How can you carve out time from your daily grind to relax and truly enjoy the little pleasures that life offers?

"I got no financial conscience; can't worry where it went.
A lasting treasure or a moment of pleasure—worth it every cent."

Spending Money (1999)

Embracing a carefree attitude towards finances, this senti-
ment highlights the joy of living in the moment. Whether
spending on a lasting treasure or a fleeting pleasure, every
cent spent brings its own kind of happiness. It's about valu-
ing the experiences and moments that make life enjoyable,
without constantly worrying about the financial cost. This
approach encourages you to find a balance between respon-
sibility and indulgence, allowing yourself to savor the plea-
sures that make life rich and memorable.

How can you enjoy the present and make the most of your
experiences rather than being tied solely to your finances?

"According to my watch the time is 'now.' The past is dead and gone. Don't try to shake it, just nod your head. Breathe in, breathe out, move on."

Breathe In, Breathe Out, Move On (2006)

The best time to live is right now. The past is behind you, and it's time to embrace the present. Instead of dwelling on what's already happened, acknowledge it, take a deep breath, and let it go. This sentiment encourages living fully in the moment, appreciating the here and now, and finding joy in moving forward. It's about recognizing that each moment is an opportunity for happiness and growth.

How can you focus on the present, embracing each day with a sense of peace and contentment, while leaving the past where it belongs?

"Therapy is extremely expensive; poppin' bubble wrap is radically cheap. You choose which one helps with your problem. I'm gonna get some sleep."

I Don't Know and I Don't Care (1999)

Sometimes, the simplest solutions are the most effective. While therapy can be costly, the joy of popping bubble wrap offers a radically cheap and fun alternative for stress relief. This light-hearted sentiment highlights the importance of finding what works best for you to unwind and address your problems. Whether it's indulging in a quirky stress-buster like bubble wrap or opting for a good night's sleep, taking time for self-care is crucial.

Embrace the little things that bring you comfort and peace. How can you find simple, affordable ways to relax and prioritize your well-being amidst life's pressures?

"Here we are, maybe it's because in spite of all the work we do, it's the child in us we really value."

Here We Are (2006)

Despite all the hard work and responsibilities, it's the child within us that we truly cherish. This sentiment reflects the importance of maintaining a sense of playfulness and wonder throughout our lives. In the midst of daily routines and challenges, nurturing our inner child brings joy and balance. Taking a break to indulge in fun and carefree moments helps us reconnect with that playful spirit.

How can you embrace the carefree, joyful side of life more often, finding happiness in simple pleasures and allowing yourself to unwind and enjoy the present? Celebrating this inner child can bring a sense of freedom and happiness, creating moments of relaxation and joy that refresh your spirit.

"The best the times can still somehow be found.
Even the worst of beaches will never let you down."

Colour of the Sun (2013)

The best times can always be found even on the worst of beaches. It's about appreciating the little things and finding moments of peace and pleasure, no matter where you are.

Embracing this laid-back attitude helps us find joy in the simple pleasures and make the most of every moment, even in imperfect situations. How can you cultivate this mindset in your daily life, finding contentment and happiness in the little moments that make life special?

"Well, the birds got me thinkin' 'bout going day drinkin'—a hall pass to be the old me. Don't need hops and barley to throw a little party. Señorita, una mas iced tea!"

The Devil I Know (2020)

Sometimes the little things, like a sunny day and a carefree moment, can inspire us to reconnect with our joyful, spontaneous side. It doesn't take much to create a moment of celebration—just a simple drink and a relaxed mindset. This sentiment encourages us to embrace the small pleasures in life and take a break from our daily routines.

How can you find and savor those moments of simple joy, letting them bring happiness and lightness to your day?

"From the music and the people to the cookin' and the joy.
It really ain't a mystery; I just followed my dancin' feet
to the University of Bourbon Street."

University of Bourbon Street (2023)

Life's pleasures can be found in the music, the people, and the simple joys around us. It's not a mystery; sometimes, you just need to follow your instincts and embrace the fun. Whether it's enjoying good food, dancing to lively tunes, or savoring moments of happiness, these experiences remind us to celebrate life.

How can you create your own moments of joy and relaxation, finding happiness in the everyday and making time to truly enjoy it?

"Feels like we're the only ones to see the morning sun, sleepin' through the afternoon and risin' with the moon. Oh don't the stars look bright."

Ragtop Day (1984)

When Friday evening rolls around, it's time to let go of the week's stresses and dive into the weekend. Slipping into your favorite clothes and blasting some rock 'n' roll, you embrace the freedom of a carefree ragtop day. Cruising around with your loved one, you relish in the joy of spontaneous adventures—dining, dancing, and watching a drive-in movie. The night stretches into morning, making you feel like the only ones awake to see the sunrise, and the stars shine brighter as you savor these moments.

How can you capture the essence of these carefree times, allowing the simple joys and spontaneous adventures to rejuvenate your spirit?

"Fuel the jet now, don't delay. Bucket lists are just cliché. No acts of contrition or asking for permission. You'll have lots of options this way."

Live, Like It's Your Last Day (2020)

Embrace the spirit of spontaneity and seize the moment without hesitation. Life's too short for endless bucket lists and waiting for the perfect time. By letting go of the need for permission or apologies, you open yourself up to countless possibilities and adventures.

How can you adopt a more carefree attitude, diving into experiences and opportunities as they come, and truly living in the moment?

"I stopped searching for perfection many waves ago.
What really matters is the here and now, and that's about all I know."

Oldest Surfer on the Beach (2013)

Embracing the present moment brings more joy and peace than chasing an unattainable ideal. This shift in focus highlights the importance of living fully in the moment and finding contentment in the simple pleasures of life. The wisdom of letting go and being present allows for a richer, more fulfilling experience.

How can you let go of the pursuit of perfection and immerse yourself in the present, discovering happiness in the everyday experiences that truly matter? By focusing on the here and now, you can cultivate a deeper sense of peace and appreciation for the world around you, making each day a meaningful part of your journey.

"Sunrise to sunrise, it's a game; 24 hours doesn't change. No point to beg, steal, or borrow from tomorrow. Whatever we need, we have it. Let's not get stuck in traffic."

Oceans of Time (2020)

How can you live fully in the moment, appreciating the abundance of what you have right now, and avoid the unnecessary rush and stress?

By focusing on the here and now, you can find peace and contentment in each day. Cherishing the simple pleasures and not worrying about what tomorrow holds allows you to make the most of every moment. It's about realizing that today's opportunities and joys are enough and finding fulfillment in the present. How can you simplify your approach to life and truly savor each day, creating a more relaxed and joyful existence?

He Went to Paris

Life's journey is marked by deep reflections and personal growth. This section delves into introspection and the wisdom gained from life's experiences.

These quotes invite you to reflect on personal growth, the importance of authenticity, and the value of life's lessons. Whether it's understanding the past, embracing change, or finding your true self, these reflections offer guidance and insight. Let these quotes inspire you to embark on your own journey of self-discovery, with the courage to live authentically and the wisdom to appreciate the path you've traveled.

"Some of it's magic, some of it's tragic,
but I had a good life all the way."

He Went to Paris (1973)

Life is a blend of magic and tragedy, each experience contributing to the rich tapestry of our existence. This sentiment captures the essence of a life well-lived, acknowledging both the highs and lows. The magical moments bring joy and wonder, while the tragic ones offer lessons and depth. Together, they create a fulfilling journey.

Embrace the full spectrum of your experiences, for they shape who you are and add meaning to your story. Reflecting on this balance helps us appreciate the beauty in both the good and the bad. How can you celebrate the magic and find wisdom in the tragedy, ensuring you live a life that feels complete and rewarding?

"Wrapped up in the problems of the day, just remember there's no re-wind and no replay. Don't you worry cause it ain't gonna fix a thing."

Lucky Stars (1999)

Even when everything seems to be falling apart, there's so-lace in cherished memories and shared experiences. This quote speaks to the enduring power of intimate moments and personal stories that bind us together, even in tough times. It reminds us that no matter how chaotic life gets, the simple, heartfelt connections we make with others remain a source of comfort and strength.

Reflect on a moment with a loved one that brings you peace and joy. How can these treasured memories help you navigate through challenging times?

"The rumors and the stories of my past, I can't deny.
I'm no St. Ignatius, but again I'm no barfly."

Bank of Bad Habits (1995)

Acknowledging our past, with all its imperfections, is a key part of self-acceptance. This lyric highlights the balance between owning up to our mistakes and recognizing that we are more than our flaws. It's a reminder that we don't have to be saints to be good people.

Reflect on your own journey and the stories that shape you. How have you grown from your experiences? Embrace your past without letting it define you entirely. Understand that being human means having a mix of virtues and vices, and it's this blend that makes you unique and whole.

"Where you gonna be when it hits the fan? Got a plan?
What you gonna do if it lands on you? Where's your point of view?"

Waiting for the Next Explosion (1999)

Life's unexpected challenges can test our preparedness and resilience. This lyric urges us to think ahead and consider how we'll handle tough situations. It's a call to develop a plan and solidify our perspectives before crises hit.

Reflect on how you respond to unexpected events. Do you have a plan in place for when things go wrong? Consider your point of view and how it shapes your actions in difficult times. Today, take a moment to prepare yourself mentally and emotionally for life's uncertainties. A little foresight can make all the difference when you face the unexpected.

"Don't try to describe the ocean if you've never seen it.
Don't ever forget that you just may wind up being wrong."

Mañana (1978)

This lyric reminds us of the importance of firsthand experience and humility. It's easy to make assumptions or pass judgments without truly understanding a situation. Acknowledging our limitations and being open to learning can lead to greater wisdom and empathy.

Reflect on a time when you made assumptions without full knowledge. How did it change once you gained firsthand experience? Today, practice humility and curiosity. Seek to understand before making conclusions, and remember that it's okay to be wrong. Embrace the opportunity to learn and grow from every experience.

"She claimed in a loud voice to be a dancer, but I don't think she's cut a rug in years. Listens to the jukebox for her answers. Slowly guzzles 25 cent beers."

Woman Going Crazy on Caroline Street (1976)

Sometimes, we hold onto identities and dreams from our past, even if they no longer fit who we are. This lyric highlights the tension between who we once were and who we've become. It's a reminder to check in with ourselves and ensure we're living authentically, not just clinging to old stories.

Reflect on the identities and dreams you hold dear. Are they still true to who you are today? How can you honor your past while embracing your present self? Consider what it means to live genuinely and let go of outdated narratives. Seek your answers not from the past, but from your current reality.

"Blame your DNA; you're a victim of your fate.
It's human nature to miscalculate."

Permanent Reminder of a Temporary Feeling (1999)

We all make mistakes, sometimes feeling like they're written in our DNA. This lyric reminds us that missteps and errors are part of being human. Accepting our imperfections can help us grow and move forward with more wisdom and grace.

Reflect on the times you've made miscalculations and how they've shaped you. How can you learn from these experiences without being too hard on yourself? Today, embrace your human nature, understanding that it's okay to stumble. Each misstep is an opportunity to learn and evolve. Give yourself the grace to miscalculate and the courage to keep going.

"Ah but the lady's not with us, she died long ago. And they don't show her movies on late midnight shows, 'cause the kids would get restless, and the grown-ups would snore. 'Cause they don't dance like Carmen no more."

They Don't Dance Like Carmen No More (1973)

Time has a way of fading memories and legends into the past. The lady who once lit up the screen no longer graces late-night shows, as her allure is lost on the younger generation and forgotten by the old. The world moves on, leaving behind a time when elegance and flair defined the dance.

This reflection captures the bittersweet nostalgia of realizing that some things, once cherished and admired, are no longer appreciated or remembered. How can you honor the memories and traditions that shaped your life, even as the world continues to change?

"He don't have no tamborine, guitar, or slide trombone. The music we make here on earth—the words they are his own."

God Don't Own a Car (1975)

True artistry isn't always about the instruments or tools we use; it's about the unique voice we bring to the world. This lyric reminds us that the beauty and meaning in our lives come from a higher power, whose influence is felt through the words and music we create on earth.

Reflect on how you express yourself and the unique contributions you bring to the world. Today, focus on the power of your own voice and story. You don't need fancy tools to make an impact—your authentic self is more than enough. Embrace the music you create with your own words and experiences, and let them resonate with those around you.

"The sky turns blue and the sun appears, but the question's still what are we doin' here. I don't think the answer's close at hand."

Barefoot Children (1995)

Even in the clarity of a new day, existential questions linger. This lyric reflects the ongoing quest for meaning and purpose, reminding us that some answers are elusive and take time to uncover. It's a reminder to be patient with ourselves as we navigate life's big questions.

Reflect on your own journey of seeking purpose. How have you approached these existential questions? Today, embrace the uncertainty and the beauty of not having all the answers. Understand that it's okay to live with questions and to seek meaning gradually. Trust that with time and experience, clarity will come, even if the answers aren't immediately apparent.

"I ate the last mango in Paris. Took the last plane out of Saigon. Took the first fast boat to China, and Jimmy there's still so much to be done."

Last Mango in Paris (1985)

These words capture the adventurous spirit of Captain Tony, the legendary owner of Captain Tony's Saloon in Key West. Known for his larger-than-life personality and boundless zest for life, Captain Tony epitomized the essence of living fully and embracing every opportunity that came his way. His journeys were filled with unforgettable experiences and stories. Yet, despite all his adventures, there was always a sense that the world held even more possibilities.

This quote serves as a reminder to us all: no matter how much we've seen or done, there's always more to explore, more to experience, and more to achieve. In the spirit of Captain Tony, let's continue to seek out new horizons and live each day with a sense of wonder and adventure.

"Fortune teller's full of gossip and news; the tattooed man is wearing his points of views. Under the big top is where we all belong—just a good vibe tribe happy to sing along."

Big Top (2009)

This lyric captures the vibrant and eclectic spirit of the Parrothead community. It's a celebration of belonging to a group that finds happiness in singing along and sharing stories.

Being Parrothead means embracing the quirky and unconventional. It's about tailgating and partying with fellow fans who understand the joy of living life to the fullest. The vibe is one of acceptance and camaraderie.

Reflect on the times you've spent with this colorful community, sharing laughs and creating memories. Today, embrace the Parrothead spirit by connecting with your fellow misfits. Celebrate the joy of being part of a community that welcomes everyone with open arms and a song in their heart.

"Go back to the country—no he really can't do that. Wasted years have left him nothing but an old straw hat, so he puts it on his head and waves a last good-bye. No time left to turn around, and no time to ask why."

Ace (1975)

"Ace" tells the story of a man who has been overlooked by society,. Despite the challenges and the world leaving him behind, Ace remains a figure of quiet strength. Ace's story is one of survival in the face of adversity. He isn't bitter or sweet; he's simply a man making his way through life with what little he has left.

Reflect on the lives of those who are often overlooked and forgotten by society. How can we extend compassion and understanding to individuals like Ace, who navigate their challenges with quiet strength and dignity? Consider the ways in which we can support and uplift those around us, ensuring that no one is left behind. Today, take a moment to acknowledge the unseen struggles of others and find ways to contribute positively to their journey.

"The god's honest truth is it's not that simple. It's the Buddhist in you; it's the Pagan in me; it's the Muslim in him; she's Catholic ain't she? It's the born again, look; its the WASP and the Jew; tell me what's goin' on, I ain't got a clue!"

Fruitcakes (1994)

Navigating the complexities of life and faith can be incredibly challenging. Reflect on the different perspectives you encounter in your own life. How do these varied viewpoints shape your interactions and understanding of the world? Seek to understand rather than judge, and appreciate the unique contributions each brings to our collective experience.

Strive to listen and learn from others, recognizing that while we may come from different backgrounds and hold different beliefs, we all share the human experience. By fostering empathy and open-mindedness, you can build bridges of understanding and navigate the complexities of life with greater clarity and compassion.

"Are we destined to be ruled by a bunch of old white men who compare the world to football and are programmed to defend? I'd like to try a princess or a non-terrestrial who is neither boast nor bashful, is there really such a girl?"

Only Time Will Tell (1996)

The lyric questions the traditional leadership dominated by old white men who view the world through a narrow lens. It expresses a desire for a different kind of leader—perhaps a princess or a non-terrestrial—someone who embodies balance and humility, free from the typical bravado.

Reflect on the qualities you believe are essential in a leader. How do these attributes compare to those of the current leadership? Imagine a world where leaders are chosen for their wisdom, compassion, and ability to unite rather than divide. Embrace the idea that true progress comes from breaking away from old paradigms and being open to new and innovative leadership that transcends traditional boundaries. By valuing diversity and inclusivity, we can work towards a future that is more equitable and just for all.

"Yeah, but now I'm gettin' old, don't wear underwear. I don't go to church, and I don't cut my hair, but I can go to movies and see it all there—just the way that it used to be."

Pencil Thin Mustache (1974)

With age comes a wonderful freedom to live life on your own terms. No longer bound by societal expectations, there's joy in embracing personal comfort and authenticity. Whether it's forgoing underwear, skipping church, or letting your hair grow wild, these choices reflect a deeper understanding of what truly matters.

Yet, amid these changes, some things remain delightfully constant, like the magic of movies that transport us back in time. This sentiment celebrates the balance between evolving with age and holding onto cherished traditions. How do you find joy in the unique blend of new freedoms and old comforts as you journey through life?

"And that's why it's still a mystery to me why some people live like they do. So many nice things happenin' out there, they never even seen the clues."

Migration (1974)

Life is full of wonders and opportunities, yet it's a mystery why some people miss out on them. There's a world of nice things happening all around, but many never see the clues. This sentiment speaks to the importance of being present and aware, of noticing the small joys and hidden treasures in our daily lives. It's a gentle reminder to open our eyes and hearts to the beauty and potential that surrounds us.

Embrace the curiosity and mindfulness that allow you to see and appreciate life's little miracles. How can you become more attuned to the positive things happening around you, ensuring you don't miss out on the subtle clues of happiness and opportunity?

"Now I used to go crazy for days at a time. Now I'm takin' my time with my days. Haven't found the answers like some that I know, I'm just stuck in a fairly nice maze."

Stranded on a Sandbar (1979)

Our journey evolves over time, shifting from the wild, carefree days to a more measured, reflective pace. There's beauty in taking your time and savoring each day, even without having all the answers. This sentiment highlights the wisdom in accepting life's uncertainties and finding contentment in the present moment.

Instead of seeking definitive solutions, it's about enjoying the journey, even if it feels like a maze. Embrace the twists and turns, and appreciate the peaceful moments within this 'fairly nice maze.' How can you find joy in the journey and make peace with the unknowns in your life?

"Jesus if I had to quit tonight, I'd never know if I was wrong or right, but that's just what you get. You gotta go the distance if you're gonna fight a good fight."

The Good Fight (1981)

Life is filled with uncertainties, and the fear of not knowing if you're right or wrong can be overwhelming. Yet, true strength lies in the willingness to go the distance and fight the good fight. This sentiment underscores the importance of perseverance and resilience, reminding us that commitment and determination are essential, even when doubt looms large. It's through these efforts that we find meaning and achieve personal growth.

Embrace the challenges, push forward, and trust in the journey. How can you apply this steadfast resolve to your own pursuits and overcome the uncertainties that come your way?

"Not long ago they criticized, the genius only wrote.
And now they listen spellbound with lumps caught in their throats."

Ain't He a Genius (1970)

Reflecting on the journey of creativity and recognition, this sentiment captures the transformation from criticism to admiration. Once dismissed, the genius now captivates audiences, leaving them spellbound and emotional. It speaks to the resilience and perseverance required to pursue one's passion despite initial doubts and naysayers.

This quote reminds us that true talent and dedication will eventually shine through, touching hearts and minds. How can you stay committed to your creative endeavors and trust that your efforts will one day be recognized and valued?

"Simple words can become clever phrases, and chapters could turn into books. Yes, if I could just get it on paper—but it's harder than it ever looks."

If I Could Just Get It On Paper (1982)

The beauty of transforming simple words into clever phrases and chapters into books captures the essence of creativity and reflection. The desire to put thoughts on paper is a quest for clarity and understanding, yet it often proves more challenging than it seems. This sentiment highlights the struggle and reward of articulating life's experiences and emotions.

It's a reminder of the power of written expression in making sense of our journey. How can you harness the power of writing to reflect on your experiences and bring clarity to your thoughts and emotions?

"I told them how we'd learned to change our sword blades into plows. I told them they should learn from us.
What should I tell them now?"

The Missionary (1970)

Reflecting on the profound changes and unexpected conflicts encountered upon returning home, this sentiment speaks to the disillusionment of finding a world at war after years spent fostering peace and understanding.

The harsh reality of returning to find leaders proud of their violence leaves one questioning what message to impart now. It captures the struggle of reconciling past ideals with present turmoil. How can you adapt your message of peace and transformation to inspire and guide others in times of unexpected conflict?

"Did you ever just want to lay down tell the world you've had enough? Did you ever just want to drop out when the goin' got a little bit rough?"

Rockefeller Square (1975)

Reflecting on the moments of exhaustion and weariness, this sentiment captures the universal feeling of wanting to lay down and declare that you've had enough. The urge to drop out when the going gets rough speaks to the challenges and pressures of life. It's a reminder of the importance of acknowledging these feelings and finding ways to rest and recharge.

How can you recognize and honor your need for a break, allowing yourself the time to recover and find strength to continue?

"It's a hell of a time to be thinking about heaven. Didn't you forget the golden rule? You've been acting like Jesus owes you a favor, but he's a little smart for you to fool."

The Christian (1970)

Contemplating lofty ideals amidst life's challenges, this sentiment serves as a poignant reminder of humility and perspective. Reflecting on the irony of thinking about heaven while forgetting the golden rule, it critiques the entitlement and the folly of trying to outsmart divine wisdom. This wake-up call encourages a return to core values and a more grounded approach to life. It's a reminder that genuine wisdom and perspective are essential, especially when navigating difficult times.

How can you maintain humility and stay true to your principles, even when life tests your resolve?

"Be good and you will be lonesome. Be lonesome and you will be free. Live a lie and you will live to regret it."

That's What Living Is to Me (1988)

This sentiment explores the paradoxes of life and the choices we make. Being good might lead to loneliness, but loneliness can bring a sense of freedom. Living a lie, however, is certain to lead to regret. These reflections underscore the importance of authenticity and the courage to embrace the complexities of life. It's a reminder to stay true to yourself, even when the path is challenging.

How can you navigate the delicate balance between societal expectations and personal freedom, ensuring you live without regret?

"Had a dream last night—took a time traveling ride back to my childhood where those monsters reside. They snack on innocence and dine on self-esteem, but I like to be in touch with what makes me scream."

Vampires, Mummies and the Holy Ghost (1994)

In a dream, you journey back to your childhood, a place where old fears still linger. These monsters feast on innocence and self-esteem, reminding you of past vulnerabilities. Yet, there's a certain strength in reconnecting with these memories and understanding what once made you scream. Embracing these moments can offer profound insights and healing.

How can you reflect on your past, acknowledging the fears that shaped you, and find empowerment in facing them head-on? By confronting these memories, you pave the way for growth and resilience.

"I'm all done explaining or passin' some test, so pour me another, it's good for my health. I'm not ready to put the book on the shelf."

Book on the Shelf (2020)

After years of meeting expectations and passing tests, there comes a time to simply enjoy life's pleasures. Another drink sounds perfect—it's good for the soul. Not ready to close the book on adventures just yet, this sentiment captures the wisdom of embracing life fully at any age.

How can one maintain their curiosity and zest for life, ensuring each day is lived to the fullest? By savoring every moment and refusing to settle, the journey remains rich and meaningful.

Keep the
Party Going!

About Beach Bum Books

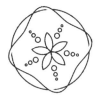

Beach Bum Books is your ultimate destination for sun-soaked stories and tropical tales. We're all about the laid-back, beach bum lifestyle, bringing you captivating reads that whisk you away to sandy shores and sunny skies.

Whether you're lounging by the ocean, dreaming of your next seaside escape, or simply looking for a moment of paradise in your day, we've got you covered. Plus, a portion of proceeds from all Beach Bum Books sales supports Save the Manatee, Mr. Jimmy Buffett's nonprofit organization.

So, grab your favorite beach chair, sip a tropical drink, and get ready to escape with Beach Bum Books—where every page is a step closer to paradise.

Printed in Great Britain
by Amazon